Legendary Lawman: Johannes F. Spreen

Legendary Lawman: Johannes F. Spreen

DR. DIANE HOLLOWAY

iUniverse, Inc.
New York   Bloomington

iUniverse books may be ordered through booksellers or by contacting:

iUniverse
1663 Liberty Drive
Bloomington, IN 47403
www.iuniverse.com
1-800-Authors (1-800-288-4677)

ISBN: 978-1-4401-1517-2 (pbk)
ISBN: 978-1-4401-1518-9 (ebk)

Printed in the United States of America

iUniverse rev. date: 1/6/2009

This book is dedicated to Elizabeth Diane Spreen, also known as "Princess Running Late," who urged the author to write a book about her father.

Princess Running Late

Preface

My Dad is my hero. He is an extraordinary human being who has accomplished so many amazing things in his life, and who continues at age 89 to contribute and live a fulfilling life with my wonderful stepmom Sallie.

Dad is a man of vision, integrity, courage, faith, compassion, silliness, strength, gentleness, justice, and is the best man I will ever know.

He's also "just my Dad", in the sense that beyond all of his triumphs and accomplishments, he's always been my Dad. I have always known I was loved, protected, and safe and cherished by both my Dad and my Mom. I came from good stock and I know it deeply. I cherish my heritage, my ancestors, my immediate family of the three of us—Dad, Mom and I—that was my world, my life, and my little universe no matter what.

No, it was not easy, but it was always blessed. Dad has walked through the fire so many times, has wrestled with heartache, betrayal, death of beloved family and dear friends, political turmoil, and even self-doubt. I know because I was there!

He has also had to wrestle with me about the choices I have made in my life, which were sometimes far less than he had hoped for me. But through my mistakes and failures, he has always been there for me, assuring me that no matter what, he loves me and will help me and still believe in me. He cherished me.

That is my foundation…my Mom and Dad are my foundation along with God, my family and friends…and my little world of three, and now Sallie as the fourth person in my little universe. She is amazing, just like Mom was. The best compliment I can give her is this:

"If I couldn't have Mom for my whole life, I am glad you are here for me, too." Sallie has enriched Dad's life so much. They will be married twenty years in December. And she is such an important person, part of my life, too. My Godmother, Aunt Doris (Doris Corrigan) is also a major influence in my life, my Mom's sister. She and Sallie have become dear friends. How cool is that? Life is good.

Dad says he's not sure about God, but let me assure you, my Dad lives a more Christian life than most anyone I know! That's the funny part—he lives God's precepts, keeps His commandments, is one of God's best ambassadors on earth, and still Dad says he's not quite sure. Let me tell you a little secret. God is sure! Ha-ha!

Dad is one of God's secret weapons, fighting for justice, keeping strong in his integrity no matter what, always loving and giving and kind to those he loves, and funny and playful like a little kid, too. Dad has no idea of what I will write for my part in this book...so I get to surprise and honor him as he did for me when he dedicated his first book to me and actually wrote it as a series of letters to me.

He laughed when I cried upon receiving my autographed copy... What a legacy to me... He laughed and said, "Honey, everyone knew but you that I was writing it this way. Ha-ha.!"

My Dad is a complex person. That's what happens when you are brilliant, inspired, capable and passionate about what you believe in. He came from humble, difficult, courageous and adventurous beginnings.

Born September 28, 1919, in Osterholz-Sharmbech, Germany, to Fredrick and Meta Spreen, Johannes Fredrick Spreen came into the world unaware of the startling adventures he would experience. He had two older siblings, big brother Henry and big sister Johanna "Hanny". The funny part of this name is in German—"Johannes" means "little John." Well, my father is 6'4 ½ inches and averages 250 pounds or so in his adult years.

When he was four, the family came to America to begin a new life. He came across the water on the *S.S. Seydlitz* and came in through Ellis Island. His name is now engraved on the Wall of Honor there. That was one of my better birthday gifts to him. He and Sallie have visited Ellis Island and have seen his name there.

I could write Dad's life history as best I know it. However, that is what this book is about! Dad's dear friend, Diane Holloway, called me for my thoughts on Dad, his life, our life, as a family, so I'll return to that here. She also said to mention the tough stuff, too, the times when things were not fun or easy. Well, every life has pain, difficulty, trouble... Everyone walks through those things in different experiences. We all hurt deeply; we all question and challenge and rebel and forgive and hopefully, eventually find our peace and heal.

The hard part for me with Dad was he was always busy, and he was gone a lot. When I was really little, I remember there was a time I didn't see him all that much. He'd be gone before I got up and I'd be in bed before he got home. However, he did always try to make time for me whenever he could.

He taught me all the sports: baseball, football, swimming, tennis, ice skating, skiing... (remember, I'm the only kid) so I was the oldest, middle, youngest, the twin, and the boy. So I got to learn everything.

Dad was my coach and my playmate. The toughest part about being an only child is that there is no one else to blame things on.

Mom knew when Dad and I were "being bad." One of my favorite memories is as follows:

Dad likes beer and would have one or two during dinner. Sometimes he had cans of beer (poured into a pilsner glass or cold beer mug) with the metal "pop tops". Remember those? Well, one night after we finished eating, Dad rolled up a little piece of napkin into a ball and used the pop-top to "fire" it at me...Of course, he was laughing, too. Well, being his kid, I had to "shoot" back. Well, you can imagine as the "battle" continued with us laughing so hard and shooting little napkin balls across the dining room table at each other... My mom was not amused. She finally said, "I give up, you two," and left the table, while we continued until we couldn't laugh any harder. Mom was a great sport. She knew she had two kids on her hands.

My Mom. Mom was Dad's partner, and biggest support. Her belief in him was the fuel to his fire. Her constant faith and encouragement enabled him to do amazing things. She was an amazing woman in her own right. She was beautiful, intelligent, brave, loving, feisty, mischievous, elegant, and faithful beyond words. She was Dad's strength. And she would also challenge him if she felt we was wrong.

They did fight (verbally only) and that scared me. They had some "knock down drag out" fights…but they *always* made up, perhaps better and stronger than before. I firmly believe good, honest arguments "fights" are an essential part of a healthy relationship. You have to love someone enough to tell them the truth, to disagree, to discuss, to argue (even loudly) and to reach resolution together.

It's rare to find someone you can fight/argue with and you know will love you enough to finish it. They had a good marriage, but it was not always easy for either one of them. But they loved each other deeply, and were always faithful to each other, and to me.

I am fortunate to say I never have seen my father drunk. I only saw him "tipsy" once. That was at home, the last night as police commissioner of Detroit…one of the hardest things for him. He loved that city. He made a huge difference for the better in only 17 months. (People still remember Commissioner Spreen in a positive way.) And he wanted to do more. I remember Mom playing Dad's song, "My Way" by Frank Sinatra for him on the record player, and putting her arms around him to embrace him as he shed a few tears. It was a poignant moment. It was also one of the few times I'd ever seen my Dad cry. And Mom was there to be his strength and to comfort him with her strongest love. I will never forget that moment…and my whole life is filled with unforgettable, amazing moments because of my Dad and Mom and the people who have filled our lives with friendship and love.

It's really hard to write about Dad in a short form. I could write volumes…heartaches Dad has known…from having lost so many beloved family members and friends of the years. Joys Dad has known, too. Accomplishments too numerous to mention here. Challenges. Adventures. Struggles Doubt. Fear. Vision. Courage. Deep love. Humor. Creativity. Strength—spiritual, mental and physical. Beauty. All of these describe things precious to Dad that have been and are hallmarks of his most amazing journey. And he's not done yet.

He has always been an amazing athlete—always from a young man as star pitcher to hundreds of medals for the Senior Olympics. Dad always believed in the mantra "sound mind, sound body." Dad is also a great philosopher and student of life. He has studied all of his life to learn as much as he can about how to achieve his goals. Whether it be hanging wallpaper, playing tennis, or studying to rise higher in the ranks of the New York City Police Department. Dad is a perennial student, even to this day. Always searching all new answers. Always posing new questions. He is s student of Life! And he is a great teacher as well.

Of course, he had expectations for me. But he has always made me feel loved and safe. And now he tells me how very proud he is of me…and that continues to astonish me. Dad and Mom left me some big footsteps to follow (Mom might not say she did, but let me assure you, she did!) And all I have ever wanted to do was to honor them for all they have done for me. (My first love and deepest commitment is to God, my Lord and good shepherd and Savior, next to my folks, just to be clear, then to all the rest of my family like my grandparents (both sides) and my Godmother and now Sallie, too. But to find now, at age 50, that Dad is proud of the woman I have become, well, it just doesn't get any better or deeper in my heart than that, because it's like hearing Mom say it, too. And that's all I've ever wanted; truly!

I love my Dad with all my heart and soul, and all that I am. His wisdom and example led me every day. Quotes he has shared with me over the years live in my memory and into my work. Quotes like "Nulle carborundum bastardos" which means, "Never let the bastards wear you down." He wouldn't tell me what that translated as until I was old enough to hear it, ha ha! And another favorite, "Success is where preparation meets opportunity at the crossroads." Another, "It's a challenge, and opportunity, and an adventure," regarding Detroit and other new adventures. And each "Gun, shield, fountain pen, comb, wallet, key?" every day before going to work as a cop in the New York Police Department. Or this favorite tongue twister, which we still laugh over when we practice it: "A box of biscuits—a box of mixed biscuits—and a biscuit mixer." Three times fast, of course! And the one that always makes him laugh and blush, "One smart fellow, he felt smart" "two smart fellows…three smart fellows…up to ten smart fellows" fast. You try it, and picture Dad laughing and blushing like a little kid!

Elizabeth Diane Spreen

Illustrations

Contents

Dr. Diane Holloway

Introduction

I met Johannes F. Spreen in the twilight of his life when he was 84 years old. He was a colossus of 6'5", a superb tennis player, an eloquent speechmaker in the Toastmasters' Club, memory teacher and exercise guru for seniors, and a spellbinding raconteur. He could hold an audience with his dynamic personality even then. He introduced himself remarking that he had been the police commissioner of Detroit at its worst crisis and followed that by being sheriff of a Michigan county for twelve years. He astonished me when this articulate gentleman said that he had never written a book but wanted to commence and needed a little assistance since he didn't have a computer.

I checked him out on Google. The man was famous. Politicians, press, police, and criminal justice authorities sought his opinions. Who was this person and what did he have to say, I wondered. Thus began an adventure into the intellect of undoubtedly the most brilliant man I have ever known.

I have been honored to assist Johannes (friends call him John) in writing several books about his career, his thoughts, and his predictions. As his energy declines, it is now my privilege to elucidate the contributions of this remarkable legendary lawman.

Dr. Diane Holloway

CHAPTER ONE:
Out of the Frying Pan and Into the Fire

On July 23rd, 1967, baseball fans turned on their television to see the Detroit Tigers play the New York Yankees at the Tiger Stadium. Johannes Spreen, a retired New York cop, couldn't miss the game as the Tigers played his team, the New York Yankees.

Willie Horton and Earl Wilson were black Detroit Tiger players, but generally, black baseball players were not altogether welcome. There was a 30% unemployment rate for blacks in Detroit and it was not Lyndon Johnson's "Great Society."

Little did he know then that he, as new police commissioner of Detroit, would soon participate in a game with Willie Horton.

As people tuned in, it soon became clear that three miles away from the stadium, there was much unrest. As the game progressed, black clouds of smoke and fire appeared on the horizon, obvious to television viewers. That night, buildings and homes began burning over a 25-square mile area. Baseball concession stands closed early. Airlines cancelled flights. The Mayor appealed to the governor for help. As the upheaval multiplied, Governor George Romney sent in state troopers and then President Johnson approved sending paratroopers. Riots raged on and on creating the largest negative image for a city ever televised live.

The Detroit Riot of 1967 was the most destructive of the urban riots of the 1960s. It had important consequences for the city of Detroit, in fact, for the entire state of Michigan, which are still ongoing. Some writers have described it as the greatest tragedy of all the long succession of Negro ghetto outbursts.

Because 1967 witnessed 164 eruptions in 128 cities across the United States, much recent scholarship has suggested that it was precisely this sort of urban uprising that sounded the death knell for America's inner cities.

The Detroit tragedy was not just the deaths, injuries, looted and burned property, but also the loss of its prominent reputation as a model city in the area of race relations.

Johannes awoke on the morning of July 24, 1967, to find every television station reporting on the riot that was enveloping Detroit. The morning newspapers did not have the story yet but the evening newspapers did. Over the next four days, the horror of death and destruction in this major American city captured everyone's attention.

The riot emerged on Twelfth Street, where an after-hours club run by a group without a license, United Community League for Civic Action, was selling alcohol (even to minors) to celebrate the return of a black veteran from Viet Nam. A tip led a Detroit police sergeant to the site on Sunday morning, and officers were surprised to find over 80 people there. During the next hour, squad cars and a paddy wagon ferried the arrested to the police station but not fast enough, as a crowd began to gather.

The first day of the rebellion, Hubert Locke, then a black administrative assistant to Detroit's police commissioner, summoned several of the city's responsible black leaders. In pairs, they spread across the Tenth Precinct to implore crowds to disperse. One pair was Deputy School Superintendent Arthur Johnson and U.S. Representative John Conyers, Jr., the latter being quite popular in his district.

Authorities allowed Conyers to stand on a car with a bullhorn to beseech the crowd to dissipate. He was the wrong man. He shouted exhortations like, "We're with you but please, this is not the way to do things. Please go back to your homes."

The crowd chanted retorts such as "No, no, no! Do not want to hear it! Uncle Tom!" One man in the crowd hollered, "Why are you defending the cops and the establishment? You're just as bad as they are!" Rocks and bottles flew toward the car, one of them hitting a policeman nearby. The crowd became uglier and Johnson urged Conyers, "Let's get out of here."

Detroit Mayor Jerome Cavanagh requested Michigan State Troopers the first afternoon. Some 360 State Police Troopers arrived in the late afternoon and the National Guard committed to send troops. The Mayor issued a proclamation for a curfew from 9:00 p.m. to 5:50 a.m. Bars and theaters were ordered to be closed across the city.

By July 25th, 14 had been killed, damage was estimated at $150 million, 731 fires had broken out, over 300 were injured, 1,663 people had been arrested, and snipers, looters, pillagers, fires and devastation continued. Due to the casualties, President Lyndon Johnson ordered 4,700 Army paratroopers into Detroit riot areas Monday night as mostly black but some white snipers launched an offensive that stretched from the West Side to Grosse Point borders.

The President ordered Defense Secretary Robert McNamara to take all appropriate steps to clear away all persons engaged in acts of violence and to restore law and order. Johnson's personal emissary, Cyrus Vance, immediately ordered 1,800 federal troops to aid Michigan National Guardsmen and State and Detroit police, who were running dangerously short of ammunition in gun battles with entrenched snipers.

The nation and Johannes Spreen watched these events unfold on television and read newspapers in stunned disbelief for four days. Newsmen had to run the gauntlet of snipers and police battles and some were injured.

Pressure built in Congress by day four for a bipartisan Senate-House investigation of the riot. The President stayed in close contact with Vance, McNamara and Romney. The press reported that President Johnson slept only five hours and was awakened three times with riot reports.

Michigan Governor George Romney re-employed his original state of emergency on the fifth day and ordered a curfew to keep "spectators, gawkers and amateur photographers" from impeding the usual flow of traffic and efforts to clean and restore public facilities in the west side riot area.

President Johnson made a radio-television address to the nation the fifth evening on the subject of civil disorders. United Auto Workers President Walter Reuther pledged the help of 600,000 Detroit labor union workers in removing the scars torn in Detroit by four days of rioting.

Meanwhile, Lt. Gen. John Throckmorton, in command of federal troops in Detroit, said that he hoped to complete the job quickly and phase out the military presence.

On the sixth day, Governor Romney demanded full racial integration of metropolitan schools and open housing to prevent new riots "or something even worse."

Pulitzer Prize winner John Hersey made the notorious Algiers Motel incident during the riot famous. It occurred, according to Hersey, when policemen killed three young black men and beat up several other people at a Detroit motel the fourth night of the riot. Prostitutes and narcotics dealers frequented Algiers Motel. Two days earlier, the police had received tips that loot taken from stores in the early hours of the riot was being sold at the motel. According to Hubert Locke, later professor and Dean of the Evan School of Public Affairs at the University of Washington, five independent investigations of the Algiers Motel incident were soon underway. When its investigation was completed, William Cahalan, Wayne County prosecutor, issued first-degree murder warrants against three Detroit police officers. Warrants were issued for only two of the three deaths, because there was a possibility that one of the three deaths had occurred prior to the arrival of the police.

"For those poised for charges of police brutality, the Algiers incident became a horribly valid *cause celebre*." (Locke, p. 46). *The Inner City Voice* criticized the inquest commenting on, "…the outrageous acquittal of police officers who were charged with murdering black teenagers at the Algiers Motel during the 1967 uprising." (Thompson, p. 83) The trial of the officers who shot the teens concluded in December 1968, after Spreen had become police commissioner of Detroit.

Before the riot, Police Commissioner Girardin (a former police reporter) had ordered police not to use guns because of long-standing negative publicity about Detroit police brutality to blacks. Soon looters knew they would not be shot at and took advantage of the situation. Rocks, bottles, looting, arsonists, Molotov cocktails, snipers, and hoodlums attacked police and firemen who tried to restore order. The Fire Chief believed that arsonists telephoned some bogus reports of fires to lure his men into gun ambushes. Even black policemen were shot, including the mother of religious writer Stephanie Mitchem, who was one of the few black female Detroit cops then.

Mayor Jerome Cavanagh looked at the city from a rooftop toward the end of the riot and said it looked like Berlin in 1945.

Mayor Jerome Cavanagh surveying damage on
12th Street where the riots began.

Following the riots, absenteeism at auto plants was so high that it
nearly stopped production, but the tension among workers and super-
visors did not erupt into violence. After surveying the Detroit rubble,
Henry Ford II, chairman of Ford Motor Company, told *Automotive
News,* "It is my feeling that this country may turn out to be the laughing
stock of the world because of situations such as we've had in Detroit. I
don't think there is much point in trying to sell the world on emulating
our system and way of life if we can't even put our own house in order."

Blacks and especially black militants in every city in the nation were
watching Detroit. Would blacks find a voice they had never known before in white city councils?

After the 1967 riot, black and white support for Mayor Jerome
Cavanagh plunged. Gun sales rose dramatically from 1966 as whites
bought weapons to protect themselves. Rumors and anxiety that blacks
might do violence to whites became particularly strong in the days
after the assassination of Martin Luther King in April 1968. Mayor
Cavanagh and city leaders decided things would have to change for
Detroit to recover.

A new police commissioner was an absolute necessity and Police
Commissioner Ray Girardin agreed. Many were considered for the
position but the search committee either rejected candidates or they
declined to accept because of the "no-win" situation in Detroit. Detroit citizens proposed plans like "put more blacks on the police force,"

"serve all citizens, not just the whites," and "build rapport and trust by getting closer to those you serve."

Johannes Spreen was known for doing those things in the New York City Police Department, and teaching about them in his law enforcement courses at John Jay College for Criminal Justice. Several people submitted Spreen's name to the Detroit Search Committee.

He had a 25-year career with the New York Police Department rising to Inspector in command of Operations but retired because of the influence of politics and favoritism at the New York police executive level. He believed that administrative responsibility should stand or fall on the performance or lack of performance, not political obligations. Would riot-torn Detroit be any different from New York?

Mayor Cavanagh invited Johannes Spreen to discuss the position of Police Commissioner of Detroit, treating him to a nice lunch on a yacht on June 20, 1968. As they sipped drinks and ate cold cuts, Cavanagh described the city, its people and government, and outlined the problems and needs of the police department. He spoke frankly about the 1967 riot and scandals that had involved some police officers of high rank.

Spreen said, "I asked him what he personally wanted from the police department, and he told me simply, a fair, effective and efficient department. I questioned whether he believed the police commissioner should run the department free from political influence or interference from other city officials. He agreed that would be difficult but we shared beliefs as to police policy and objectives, and that I thought I could contribute to solving Detroit's problems. He stuck out his hand, and I shook it." As of that moment, Spreen was Detroit's police commissioner, although the people of Detroit did not know it.

The next day, the mayor announced Spreen as the new police commissioner. On July 22, one day before the anniversary of the Riot of 1967, he was sworn in as Detroit's Police Commissioner at police headquarters.

Because he had anticipated an in-and-out visit with no overnight stop, Spreen brought no additional gear with him. He and the Mayor checked their waistlines for clothing exchange and Spreen was provided an accommodation. When he appeared at the press conference the following day, he was wearing the Mayor's underwear, his shirt and tie!

Johannes called upon the retiring Detroit Police Commissioner,

Ray Girardin, at his home. The one-time career newspaperman was most generous with information about the commissioner's job, and particularly about relations with the local press. He seemed genuinely relieved that someone had finally appeared to assume the burdens of the commissioner's responsibilities.

Back at the hotel, Johannes called his wife, Elinor, and told her he was impressed with Detroit as a city, the Detroit police as a department and Mayor Cavanagh as a charismatic city official. He found her wishing that they could finally enjoy their lives free of stress and strain. He then reminded her that he wanted to put into practice the things he had learned from experience and theorized and in his classes at the New York City Police Academy and John Jay College.

The next morning, the Mayor opened a conference by saying he had scouted the entire country, and had found the best man. He introduced Spreen who stated, "I want police to think of themselves as protectors of liberty. Protecting the rights of the individual is their function. There will be no room for bias, bigotry or brutality!" He went on to promise that he would do his best to maintain a high level of crime fighting, raise the level of police performance especially in the area of professionalism, and to improve the relationship between police and the community.

When he returned to New York, the news was out and most of his friends and work associates had the same reaction: "Not Detroit!"

He then tried to bone up on information about Detroit, but had only a few days before taking command.

Was Spreen able to contribute anything to stabilize the city? What contributions did he make to law enforcement and to the lives of citizens in Michigan? What legacy did he leave to all of us in the United States?

That is the theme of this biography of Johannes F. Spreen. He made so many innovative changes as Police Commissioner of Detroit that any one of them would have been commendable. But to do it in the limited time of his term, 17½ months, and against the most resistant city council and city leaders in America at that time was nothing less than phenomenal. Then following his term as police commissioner, he brought changes into the Oakland County Sheriff's Department in Michigan that had never been seen before or since. That is why Johannes Spreen is a legendary lawman. But first, where did that man come from and how did he get to this point in life?

Chapter Two:
German Boy Rises to NYPD Executive

Johannes Spreen was born September 28, 1919, in Osterholz-Scharmbeck near Bremen, Germany. His mother, Meta Spreen, was born February 18, 1881, and died July 22, 1957. His father, Fred Spreen, was born in 1881 and died in 1963.

His parents brought him to America in 1923 when he was nearly four. His only two recollections of Germany and their little village home on 212 Hundestrasse were these. He told an older boy that he got a necktie (schlips) for Christmas but comically mispronounced it "snips", and promised to send the boy some bananas from America. The other memory was that his dog, Tell, stole some wurst (sausage) from the table and ran it up to eat in the attic. His mother, a cook at a Bremen hotel before marriage, not only made excellent wurst but also made a wonderful butterkuchen or butter cake.

Years later when Johannes and current wife Sallie visited his German home, they met the woman who bought it from his parents. She served them delicious local wine and made a gift of some beautiful crystal glasses. Johannes asked to see the attic where his dog had taken the wurst. Now a strapping 6'5", he remembered the attic ceiling as high but had to bend to get in. When he came down, he tried to make a joke about the address of this home. He said since 212 degrees Fahrenheit is water's boiling point, and Hunde means "dog" and strasse means "street", he kidded that he lived on "Hot Dog Street." The joke seemed to be lost on the hostess who reminded him that the street number meant either the 212th house built in that little village or built on that street. Oh, well, he and Sallie enjoyed their visit.

Photo of the *S.S. Seydlitz*

Johannes' brother and his father came first to America. He followed with his mother and sister on the *S.S. Seydlitz* to New York City in 1923. They were three of the 1,700 third-class passengers.

Some crewmembers of the *S.S. Seydlitz*
when Johannes sailed to America.

Johannes' brother was enumerated in Ellis Island documents as Hermann Spreen, arriving November 19, 1922, on the *S.S. Hannover* from Bremen, born in Scharmbeck, Germany, 6 feet tall, age 17, single, and was not a polygamist or anarchist. His uncle Hermann Spreen was marked as having paid for his trip. Young Hermann had $25 when he arrived in America.

Seven months later, Johannes' father arrived on June 6, 1923, having also sailed on the *S.S. Hannover* from Bremen. Ellis Island recorded him as cigar-maker Friedrich Spreen, German, last residence Scharmbeck, birthplace Westerbeck, a non-polygamist or anarchist, age 41 years, 6'3", blonde with green eyes. He had paid for the trip himself, had $25, and was to be in contact with a friend, Diedrich Horstmann, in Glendale, New York. Johannes would later recall that the first dead bodies he ever saw were Diedrich's two daughters, laid out in the house for viewing on two separate dates—a shocking experience for a child. "Why did they die so young?" he wondered.

Johannes' mother, Meta Spaeth Spreen, his sister Johanna (twelve years older than Hans) and he left Bremen on the *S.S. Seydlitz* sailing from Bremen August 13 and arriving on September 15, 1923, according to their sailing documents.

Little did passengers know that they were sailing to a country where the president, Warren G. Harding, had just died August 3, 1923, just ten days earlier. Harding was succeeded by his vice president, Calvin Coolidge. Most Europeans saw the United States as a stable land of opportunity. Rumors that a president could die under unusual circumstances such as the possible poisoning by his wife for his numerous flagrant affairs and at least one illegitimate child sounded more like European intrigues.

Johannes has often pondered why his parents came to America. He has speculated that 1923 was in the aftermath of World War I but too early for the rise of Adolf Hitler, was it because of the terrible inflation that hit Germany, or was it because of the unrest and killings of the royal family in Russia a few years earlier. The latter reason might seem unrelated to Germany but there was a time when little Johannes reasoned that his father and mother were the king and queen of a small country and had to flee—a myth many small children have when forced to move away from their homeland.

S.S. Seydlitz arrival document dated September 15, 1923.

Little Johannes was registered at Ellis Island as last residing in Osterholz, Germany. His sister, Johanna was 15, he was three, and his mother, Meta Spaeth Spreen, 42, born Worpswede, was 5'8" with green eyes and blonde hair. Their voyage was funded by Johannes' father, whom they were to join at 141 Cooper Street in Brooklyn.

These musicians entertained on the 1923 voyage of *S.S. Seydlitz*.

The *S.S. Seydlitz* pulled into Ellis Island on September 15, 1923. Johannes has two recollections of the month-long trip. He didn't recall the entertainment but remembered mounting many steps from the lower floor where third-class passengers stayed. The other memory was when a passenger hoisted the three-year-old up onto the rail and teased about chucking him into the water. He began to shriek and developed a phobia of the water which haunts him yet, despite having been a prize-winning swimmer in his youth.

Johannes doesn't remember passing the "Lady holding the Golden Torch" as they arrived in New York, but has always been grateful to his parents for coming to America. He believed that otherwise in 1936 when he reached the age of 17 (like Pope Benedict) he would have been forced to join the Hitler Youth.

Johannes and his family came to America when many countries had already exceeded their immigration quotas but Germany had not. In 1923, some 14,000 immigrants were received at Ellis Island and all were checked to be sure they would not be troublesome and were not bringing in communicable diseases--a time-consuming procedure. While awaiting their turn, he was among those served in the Immigrant Dining Room. The fare consisted of boiled eggs, milk for all women and children, beef broth with barley, boiled potatoes, vegetables, sour pickles, tapioca pudding, bread, butter, and coffee.

Ellis Island with New York City in the background in 1923.

Johannes, his sister and mother joined his father and brother. He turned four only five days after arriving in New York. He recollects a fourth-floor "railroad flat" in Brooklyn with windows in the front and rear and sidewalls flush against the adjoining tenements. All tenants on that floor shared the communal bathroom. Their home was between the cross streets of Central and Evergreen, near the borough boundary between Brooklyn and Queens, and near Evergreen Cemetery.

Their new home at 141 Cooper Street was bustling. When Johannes was five years old, a car hit him. He bled from his ear, probably due to a concussion, remembered lots of blood, and spent a short time in the hospital. He also bit his nails as a youth, which led to a severe infection. Doctors had to sever about ¾" of an inch from the middle finger on his left hand. Ever since, he advises, "Don't bite your nails."

His parents never learned to speak fluent English. He went to first grade at age six and still had a thick German accent. He learned to speak proper English but even after several years, his German accent still brought on fights until he learned to speak with a Brooklyn accent.

Both his parents used to sing and Johannes remembers a little ditty his mother sang to him, which he translated for the author:

> Hanchen klein ging alleing (Little Hans went alone) in die weite welt hinein (into the wide world).
> Stuck und hut steht im gut er ist wohl gamut (A cane and hat fit him well. He is quite happy.)
> Aber mutter weinert sehr sie hat doch kein Hanschen mehr (But mother weeps a lot—she does not have her little Hans).
> Hanschen klein, ging allein in die weite weld hinein. (Little Hans went alone into that wide world.)

And now little Hans in American has become an outstanding lawmen—a "legendary lawman."

His father continued as a cigar maker when the Great Depression started in 1929. At first, he worked for others but through effort eventually established his own cigar production. Johannes' first wife, Edna, labeled his father a "capitalist." Most people switched to cheaper smokes during the Depression, and "Fred" accommodated customers with his low prices.

Like most other families, the Spreens endured the hard times as best they could. First, they moved a few doors up to 200 Cooper Street to a ground floor home instead of a tenement. They had their own separate house and a garden and one of Johannes' happiest days was when they moved in.

Then they moved across the borough boundary into the Ridgewood section of Queens in 1934. Johannes entered Richmond Hill High School and went out for the high school baseball team, competing for the shortstop position against another teenager named Phil Rizzuto. Rizzuto became the pride of the Richmond Hills High baseball team, and went on to become the pride of the New York Yankees, being called "Scooter Rizzuto." Johannes became a pitcher.

Rizzuto was born in 1917 in Brooklyn, the son of a streetcar motorman. Despite being only 5'6", he was named the Most Valuable Player of the American League in 1950. Rizzuto later enjoyed a 40-year career as a radio/TV sports announcer for the Yankees, was inducted into the Baseball Hall of Fame in 1994, and died in 2007.

With that kind of competition, Johannes soon shifted to pitching where his height (eventually 6'5") probably intimidated batters. As a young guy, he was good in baseball, basketball, tennis, race walk, swimming, and won many medals. He graduated high school in 1937, prepared for college scholastically but not economically. The high school annual pictures showed him in many clubs, speech, baseball, basketball, handball, honor role, scholarship pins, and having edited a prize-winning class paper. He signed this annual on top of his information with "Your pal, Hans."

A faithful and good servant is a real godsend.
SPREEN, HANS FREDRIC (Slim)
Sr. Arista. Jr. Arista. Scholarship Pin. Varsity Baseball '35. Interclass Basketball '33, '34, '35, '36. Interclass Handball '33, '34. Regents Honor Roll. P. S. A. L. Pins '35, '36. Editor of Eng. 6 Prize-Winning Class Paper. Blue Cards. Speech 5H.

Entry in 1937 Richmond Hill High School Yearbook

When he was 18, a friend, Freddy Bogens Berger, said, "Let's study to become police officers." He agreed and passed the exam but Freddy didn't. Johannes had to procure his birth certificate from Germany before he could be hired. When he received it, he noted a swastika emblem on it. He was then able to obtain papers termed "Derivative Citizenship." He still spoke German at home with his parents, but thanks to them was an American citizen. His mother had always called him Hans, a short form of Johannes. He and his parents feared that his German name alone would disqualify him from becoming a New York police officer, but he continued the application process all the same.

Police candidates also had to pass a series of physical performance tests as well as a medical examination. He ran, hurdled, jumped, chinned, swung on ladder bars, and discovered that he not only passed the physical, but also achieved the highest score in the performance tests. The *New York Daily News* and the now defunct *New York Daily Mirror* ran his picture in a centerfold about new police rookies, listing him as Hans Spreen. He hated the name Hans but assumed that was his real name. He changed his name to Johannes when he entered the police department, because he had discovered from his birth certificate and ship's invoice that his true name was Johannes.

Although he had no college credit, he placed 183rd out of 22,000 applicants on the 1939 examination. On the final list of 7,000 in October, 1939, he scored second highest, following Valentine Pfaffman, a name he would never forget. However, because he was not quite 21 years old he was passed over, which was very sad for him. He had married Edna DeFliese in 1940 when both were under 21.

Spreen had applied to the New York Police *and* Fire Departments and passed both exams, but the Police Department was the first to reply. So, the first class of 300 was sworn in and appointed June 5, 1940, at the phenomenal New York World's Fair, featuring the Trylon and Perisphere structures.

The New York World's Fair opened on April 30, 1939. This world's fair is often invoked as proving to the American public that prosperity and good times lay ahead after the decade of the Great Depression. The fair included the participation of 52 nations and 11 colonies, despite the growing presence of a looming World War. The New York fair closed on October 21, 1940 but drew 45 million paid visitors. During the same year, a competing fair in San Francisco, known as the Golden Gate Exposition, became a second example of a spectacular world's fair predicting the end of the Depression years. It opened in the middle of San Francisco Bay on February 18, 1939, and closed on September 29, 1940, with attendance figures of over 15 million.

Romantic Johannes proposed to Edna on bended knee sporting a mustache to enhance his mere 20 years.

Spreen would be 21 years old on September 28th and attended the Madison Square Garden with Edna. The 1940s Graduate Show was called "Around the Clock with New York's Finest."

Mayor Fiorello LaGuardia addressed the group. Johannes' heart sank when LaGuardia announced that there would be no more appointments to the police force for five years because of the draft— the Selective Service Act. However, Johannes was fortunate because of the "Mad Dog Killings," and was hired in 1941. Two Italian guys robbed a linen company, shot the manager, and then feigned insanity (drooling, howling, barking, etc.) until their execution, creating a public outcry for more police.

His Sicilian bandmaster father, Achille LaGuardia, raised LaGuardia at Fort Whipple in Prescott, Arizona. He played the violin as a youth. He always enjoyed music and is pictured here with the famous Cuban composer, Ernesto Lecuona, who wrote "Malaguena," "Siboney," and "Always in My Heart." Lecuona and Gonzalo Roig founded the Cuban Symphony. Roig's music is the basis for the 1992 movie, "The Mambo Kings," with Armand Assante and Antonio Banderas.

Ernesto Lecuona, Gonzalo Roig, John Sperry (Lecuona's attorney) and Mayor Fiorello LaGuardia (l to r).

Johannes kept a copy of Mayor LaGuardia's 1941 speech to new police recruits. LaGuardia, portrayed in the Broadway musical *Most Happy Fella*, said,

I want to warn you; I am old in this game. I have been in

public office 37 years. I know a faker. I can smell one ten blocks away and I recognize one when I read a line he writes or hear a word he says…I was given a confidential report by an organization that made a thorough secret, scientific investigation of the Police Department with all its multiple duties. And it shows a state of efficiency and a degree of law enforcement so high and so perfect, although in a city of seven and a half million people, reflecting conditions that would do credit to a small community of 5,000 people in a rural district…

We have to sleep at night, or whenever we have off time between tours for the purpose of sleep. So never do anything that would disturb that sleep…Stick with your old friends. I know what it means. When I moved over here to this office, I could have made many new friends but my wife and I don't associate with anyone we did not associate with before I became Mayor. Stick to that! You know many people who will think that you have suddenly become a great fellow just because you now have a shield.

Live within your means. Don't try to live up to the Joneses…

Let me add another warning. You and I don't shape the foreign policies of our government. The American people have delegated that authority and power to their officials, and as members of the Police Department you will refrain from taking any active sides in any controversy concerning the foreign relations of the United States…as police officers you are not free to take any active part in politics. We stress that again and again. We mean what we say.

If at any time you feel that you cannot look into the muzzle of a gun, take up another profession, because you are assuming risks in the profession which you have chosen.

Little did Johannes know at that young age that he would be looking into the muzzle of a gun later in Florida.

Johannes enjoyed his job and also enjoyed sports. As a good pitcher, he was asked to play for the New York Police against the James Barton Night Hawks, a team in the Baseball Alliance. He was proud to recall that James Barton was the star of the play *Tobacco Road* on Broadway.

Once Spreen became a police officer in the New York City Police Department (NYPD), he stayed on that road until he reached the top, but there was a detour.

After two years as a cop, he enlisted as an aviation cadet in the U.S. Army Air Corps Cadet Program on April 30, 1943.

CADET IDENTIFICATION CARD

CADET....SPREEN, JOHANNES F.
CADET SERIAL NO. 32900366
CADET CLASS....44-7
CADET FLIGHT....G
CADET BARRACKS...291-4 P
CADET ROOM....14

AC SPREEN
BOMB

Spreen's 1943 military cadet identification card.

Because he made high scores, he became a lieutenant on May 20, 1944, and was sent to Norwich University College Training Detachment in Vermont. Only eleven cadets out of the 500 men who had arrived at Norwich University were sent to Nashville, Tennessee, for classification as a pilot, navigator, bombardier, or failure. These were the top eleven of the incoming class, but as top students they were sent on ahead to fill spaces of the class before those who were going to pre-flight school. Spreen only got six weeks of training in Vermont instead of the intended three months.

Johannes Spreen, aviation cadet at Norwich
University in Northfield, Vermont, 1944.

Because of his height (too tall to fit in a fighter jet) Johannes was assigned to instruct cadets and to fly in B-29s. He was sent to Santa Ana for pre-flight training followed by Victorville Army Air Force Base for Bombardier training. Then on May 20, 1944, he graduated, had an officer's uniform, bombardier wings, and became an instructor at Victorville. During his year at Victorville, he had a narrow escape when airplanes flew in such tight formation that a door was ripped off one of the planes.

In Victorville, Spreen pitched for his team and proudly recalled a shutout against the El Toro Marine Base. Later, he pitched a "no hitter" vs. the Las Vegas Horned Toads. A highlight was the New Year's Eve party at the Victorville Officer's Club in 1944. One of the captains was married to actress Priscilla Lane. Her sister, actress Rosemary Lane, also was there. Priscilla had a great shape and was dressed in a very fetching cat's costume. The Lane sisters were in movies such as *Four Daughters, Arsenic and Old Lace, Saboteur, Meanest Man in the World,* etc. They first sang with the Fred Waring band and entered show business where Priscilla (Pat) became a bigger star than Rosemary. On May 22, 1942, she married Air Force lieutenant Joseph Howard. The following year she gave up her show business career to follow Joe around during his military stint and often appeared in camp shows.

As a lieutenant and bombardier instructor, Johannes had a little time to play tennis in his off hours, his most enjoyable sport.

Spreen played tennis in 1944 at Victorville as lieutenant and bombardier instructor with an old wooden racquet.

Other officers at Victorville during Spreen's time were singer "Tennessee" Ernie Ford and actor Tim Holt, son of actor Jack Holt.

Tim was instrumental in getting Bob Hope to do a show in Victorville. Holt's education was at the Culver Military Academy before his show business career. Tim was a bombardier instructor, a fine man, and helpful to many. He flew 22 missions in the Pacific, the last over Tokyo on the *last* day of the war, in which he was wounded. He received a Purple Heart and the Distinguished Flying Cross. Tim starred with his father in *Treasure of Sierra Madre* with Humphrey Bogart and Walter Huston. Besides westerns, Tim was in *Back Street* with Charles Boyer, was hired by Orson Welles for *The Magnificent Ambersons*, and later appeared in *Hitler's Children* with Bonita Granville and in *My Darling Clementine* with Henry Fonda.

Tim Holt was also in *5th Ave Girl* with Ginger Rogers; *Stagecoach* with John Wayne; *Sons of the Legion* with Evelyn Keyes, William Frawley, and Donald O'Connor; *The Renegade Ranger* with Rita Hayworth; *Gold Is Where You Find It* (1938) with Olivia de Havilland and Claude Rains; *I Met My Love Again* with Joan Bennett and Henry Fonda; *Stella Dallas* with Barbara Stanwyck and *The Vanishing Pioneer* with his father and William Powell. There were even *Tim Holt* comic books. He finally left show business to be a radio station manager in Oklahoma.

Later one of the Spreen's Victorville bombardier students became a movie star. Paul Picerni from New York flew 25 combat missions and received the Air medal with three Oak Leaf Clusters and the Distinguished Flying Cross. After the military, he went to drama school where he learned to act while also being the Los Angeles Rams NFL half-time master of ceremonies for 30 years. He was in some rather forgettable movies such as *Mara Maru, Desert Song, Operation Pacific,* and *The House of Wax* with Vincent Price. He was best known for being Elliot Ness' sidekick in a television series called *The Untouchables* starring Robert Stack. He was also known as the "Benefit King" because he emceed so many banquets and benefits through the years.

Spreen recalled the fine men he served with in bombardier training as well as some memorable characters and life-long friends. Then he was sent to Lincoln, Nebraska, for B-29 training. His wife, Edna, joined him in a small apartment in someone's home. He had become disenchanted with her because of her smoking, her lying, and her in-

eptitudes but attempted to maintain the marriage. Following his training, he was sent to Harvard, Nebraska, for bombing practice runs.

His group captain was Captain Charles Navarro, brother of
Mexican silent screen star Ramon Navarro (who played the Charlton
Heston role in the original *Ben-Hur*). Charles' cousin was Mexican
silent screen actress Delores Del Rio. Charles had a wall hanging of
bulls-eye shack targets with green strings attached to each B-29 crew.
Johannes' crew string was the shortest distance (29 feet from the target)
and they were very proud of Captain Navarro. Among Spreen's many
usual military duties, he also taught German to military officers—a
show of strength.

Then the time came for the bomb group to fly to Okinawa. In
two more days, Spreen's team was to fly to a California base where
they would take off for Okinawa, in fact his footlocker had already
been sent there. Then pilot Paul Tibbetts dropped the atomic bomb
on Hiroshima from his *Enola Gay* on August 6, 1945. Johannes' crew
learned that if Tibbetts had not done so, they would probably have had
to. Johannes was relieved that as lead bombardier, he did not have to
face that moment.

Much later, Johannes' navigator, Brad Bradford, was discussing the
last days of World War II with some high school students in Highland
Park, Illinois. His talk was recorded and this information was sent to
Spreen in 2005.

> We were supposed to fly from Saipan, Japan and Guam…
> Finally, it got near the end of summer [1945], they came around
> and got $50 from each of us officers for the Officers Club on
> Okinawa, and we were finally going to get some action. For a
> squadron, that was quite a bit of money and I got to fly a B-17
> on liquor runs. We'd fly out to put it on a boat to go over to
> Okinawa so when we got there, we'd have plenty of liquor.
> My footlocker got to Okinawa. They dropped the bomb, that
> was the end… My bombardier was former policeman for the
> New York City police, Johnny Spreen, big guy, 6'4", a Dutch
> boy, and he's been a beat man. He sent back right after the war
> ended for materials for the Sergeant's exams and while we were
> goofing off, he studied for that exam for several months before

we got out. He went back to New York and was second high-est in the test. Later, he became Deputy Police Inspector of the New York Police Department, came out to Detroit and was the Detroit Police Commissioner. Then he became Sheriff of one of the counties just north of Detroit.

A student asked Brad, Do you think we should have dropped the bomb on Japan?

Brad answered: Oh, sure. No question about it. The only thing that I would have done different about it was I would have announced that we were going to drop it in an uninhabit-ed place and let them see it. However, I don't think that would have changed a thing. A lot of people were going to get killed anywhere—not just a few. Thank you for listening.

When the U.S. defeated Germany, Spreen mused that if his parents had remained in Germany, life would have been considerably differ-ent for him. He suspected that he would probably have been forced into the Hitler Youth, marching and shouting "Heil Hitler." However, thanks to his parents, he was in America. After the war, he returned to the NYPD in 1946.

Since Johannes had learned that his wife was a smoker, he decid-ed to accept it when he came home for a furlough in mid-1944. He showed Edna his new lieutenant uniform and wings. He then present-ed her with a gold cigarette case filled with cigarettes and offered her one. She was surprised that he had decided to try to save the marriage by smoking along with her. It did not work, however, and he sadly divorced her in 1946 on grounds of adultery.

He continued to smoke until his retirement from the NYPD in 1966. "Blame it on the woman," the guys used to say.

In the summer of 1947 after his divorce, Johannes was introduced to a woman with a large picture hat. Such hats always attracted his attention, and he was delighted to meet Elinor Fallon, daughter of fel-low officer Jim Fallon. Unbeknownst to Johannes, Elinor had queried another officer about the lanky fellow. She was told, "He treats a lady like a queen and a floozy likes a floozy," which attracted Elinor.

Johannes was then dating a beautiful model for the Canada Dry Ginger Ale company. They went to a party where he introduced the two women to each other. As his love for Elinor grew, he dropped the model. Johannes and Elinor romantically eloped and married in the home of a Justice of the Peace in Greenwich, Connecticut, on May 29, 1948. Greenwich was the Las Vegas of the time, a place where people went to get married.

In 1949, Johannes received a citation for arresting a man for attempted murder while on vacation with Elinor in Florida.

The Spreens moved into an apartment above Johannes' parents, and Elinor lovingly cared for his aging mother.

In one interesting aside, Elinor was inspired to become a police officer after she married Johannes. Despite a father and husband in the profession, she decided that it was not something she liked and she resigned after six months.

Spreen with a cigarette riding a bronco at Cimarron
Dude Ranch in Peekskill, New York.

Spreen, age 29 or 30, while still a Police
Academy training officer with NYPD.

Spreen became a Police Academy training officer as a lieutenant, and then reorganized and improved the Recruit Training Program. In 1954, he was selected as the first New York police officer to attend the Southern Police Institute. That nationally known professional school offered a three-month course with heavy emphasis on human relations training. Bob Tuffy was also selected to go with Spreen.

Southern Police Institute graduates of 1956.
Spreen was the first NYPD officer to attend the
3-month course. Upper row, farthest right.

Johannes finally started college at age 35 in 1954. After 12 years, he achieved a bachelor's degree, then a master's, and did considerable work on his doctorate—all but his dissertation.

After years of hard work, Johannes and Elinor bought and remodeled the home of Elinor's boss to welcome their little bundle of joy, Elizabeth Diane Spreen.

Johannes was assigned to conduct promotion courses for those preparing to be sergeants, lieutenants and captain, as well as leading seminars on police tactics and field operations for all superior officers. In 1958, he was promoted to captain, the highest rank in the New York Police Department for which a written examination was taken.

Elinor, Betty and John in his new NYPD Captain's uniform.

As she grew, Betty loved it when her daddy made up stories for her, and sometimes sang as his father had done in a choir and as his mother had sung nursery rhymes to him. A favorite story was about an Indian brave, Thundercloud, and his love, a maiden named Dancing Star. They waited a long time to have their first baby, just as Johannes and Elinor had done, and the Indians named their little one "Princess Running Late." Betty loved these glorious stories, told them to others, and was eventually stimulated to take up a career with the Renaissance Festivals. The indefatigable Johannes later proudly decided to publish his tales, illustrated beautifully by nephew Justin Rose. The book is entitled *The Saga of Thunder Cloud and Dancing Star.*

The stories describe bravery, endurance, true love, leadership, humor, a play on words, and the traits of a confident man and loving husband and father. Here are condensed versions of three of these stories.

The Buffalo Hunt

Dancing Star had noticed handsome Thundercloud, who was the son of the chief and was about to go on a buffalo hunt.

She stared at Thundercloud and walked toward him. "Thundercloud, accept this arrow pouch for your hunt," Dancing Star said. "But I wish you would not go tomorrow. You are important as our next leader and need to stay safe."

Taking the quiver from Dancing Star's shaking hand, Thundercloud said, "As a future leader, I must lead. This hunt is necessary for food for our winter months and I'm not afraid with Pal-o-mine to ride."

Later, Dancing Star ran to the edge of the village and waited for the hunters to return. Whenever a hunter returned, Dancing Star asked for news about Thundercloud. No one knew where he was.

Entering her family's teepee, she changed her dress, grabbed a small knife, a buffalo hide and fire-making supplies. She whispered to herself, "I'm going to find Thundercloud."

Soon, the sun was low in the sky, but Dancing Star still searched as night came even though she stopped many times to listen for sounds.

When a rock tumbled from a cliff overhang, Dancing Star dismounted her horse to investigate.

"Are you up there, Thundercloud?" she yelled.

"Yes, come on up and let me see your happy face."

She gasped when she spotted three gashes on Thundercloud's right leg. "What happened to Pal-o-mine and how did you get these gashes?"

"A cougar jumped at Pal-o-mine during the storm. When he whirled and reared to stomp the mountain lion, I slid off and felt on some jagged rocks," Thundercloud said.

"Did the cougar try to attack you?"

"No. He chased Pal-o-mine when he ran off. I planned to cut a walking stick and go back today, but you came instead," Thundercloud said as he chuckled.

As they both rode back on Dancing Star's horse, Thundercloud said, "Look, it's not far to our village, so I'll sing to you. I need to practice my victory song about killing two large buffaloes and the cougar attack on Pal-o-mine before our celebration tonight."

"I'll listen only if you include my search for you," Dancing Star said.

Laughing again, Thundercloud agreed and burst out singing, "On my first hunt, two buffalo I killed for meat. Then a storm came and a cougar attacked Pal-o-mine, but my horse is a fierce fighter like me and stomped the animal until it ran away..."

"Thundercloud, tell about me, too."

"Dancing Star is aptly named for she traveled at night to find me even though she was the only star about last night," Thundercloud sang.

As they entered their village, all the children yelled, "Thundercloud returns!"

Thundercloud and Dancing Star dismounted in front of Chief Power Bear's teepee.

The chief embraced his son, thanked Dancing Star, and the tribe prepared for their feast.

Picnic at the Lake

One day, Chief Power Bear said, "The young feel restless when they have nothing to do. This year, games will be played as the teepees are set up by the lake. Thundercloud and Dancing Star will conduct them. Prizes will be awarded."

The chief continued, "Dancing Star and Thundercloud will go to the lake and arrange the games."

They held hands and planned all of the games as they walked to Dancing Star's home. Before she entered the teepee, Thundercloud hugged her and whispered, "It'll be great to have you helping me with the games."

She snuggled close to him, kissed him, and then entered her home.

The next day, Thundercloud offered a horse named Two Sock Lady to Dancing Star to ride to set up the games. On their fast horses, the couple soon reached the lake. As she began to paint targets on trees, Thundercloud went to find a deer for the little ones to track. "Try to be back for lunch at noon," Dancing Star said. Soon she finished her painting. Thundercloud hadn't returned, so she spread a buffalo blanket at the edge of the lake next to a big rock. She fell asleep, but woke when she heard Pal-o-mine's pounding hoofs.

Thundercloud slid off his horse and retrieved the rabbit he'd hunted for their picnic lunch. He carried his trusty bow in his left hand.

Dancing Star sat up, and started to stand until she heard a buzzing rattle. She froze.

Thundercloud heard the sound, dropped the dead rabbit, notched an arrow and let it fly. It pierced the snake's head and pinned it to the blanket next to Dancing Star's hand. He ran toward her. She jumped up to meet Thundercloud's outstretched hands.

Holding her in a tight embrace, Thundercloud whispered, "You're safe. Quit trembling."

"Thank you, Thundercloud. You shoot straight and true. I love you. Are you going to court me at the next Full Moon?" She snuggled close to his side and kissed his cheek.

"You'll have to wait and see, but we've got to get ready for tonight's ceremony. I'll take you home for now." He reached for her hand.

The Swim at the Canyon Waterfall

Dancing Star wanted to go riding, but her mother said they needed to prepare for her wedding, two moons away. All household items, poles for a teepee, and skins to cover the poles must be completed and set up away from the village for Thundercloud and Dancing Star's honeymoon.

Finally about noon, Dancing Star's mother said, "Go for a ride and find saplings suitable for poles. Mark them with yellow paint."

Dancing Star ran to the corral, whistled for her horse, mounted and rode away toward the canyon waterfall. "A swim, that's what I need," she thought.

As soon as she heard the roar of the waterfall, she found a shade tree for her horse. Walking to the swimming hole, she heard a splash, so she stopped and listened. She snuck closer and saw Thundercloud in the pool near the waterfall. His clothes lay on a rock. She smiled, dashed to the rock, picked up his clothes, and hid them behind several large rocks nearby.

Returning, she shouted, "Ha, ha, Thundercloud! Where are your clothes?"

He swam closer to Dancing Star, treaded water, and noticed she stood on a large slanted rock. He splashed water until the rock became slippery and she fell into the water.

"Ha, ha! You're all wet, too. Now, tell me where my clothes are," Thundercloud said.

She refused, so he kept splashing until she finally said, "Okay, I'm cooled off and your clothes are behind those large rocks." She pointed.

"Hide your face," he said as he scampered out of the water.

Dancing Star did hide her face between her fingers, but kept her fingers apart a little to peek as Thundercloud rushed to the rocks, dressed, whistled for Pal-o-mine, and leaped on the horse's back. He rode straight for her horse, grabbed its reins, and left with both horses before Dancing Star got out of the water.

"Why did he do that? It's a long walk home," she thought as she started walking. By the time she walked a mile, her clothes dried. She sat in the shade of a tree and rubbed the bottoms of her feet. She stood up when she heard horses approaching.

Thundercloud dismounted. He stood by the horses and waited.

"Thank you for returning, but why did you do that?" Dancing Star asked.

"Oh, I was just *horsing around,* but I didn't want you to

walk all the way to the village, so I came back."

During the rest of their courtship, Thundercloud provided rabbits and quail every day for their afternoon meals when they went riding. Dancing Star cut and prepared hides every evening for their household. Now, tomorrow was their wedding day.

After the ceremony and feast, they wanted to leave for their honeymoon. Every day of their honeymoon, they talked, made plans to help their people, and decided how to raise the children they hoped to have.

They returned to their village and carried out their duties. Many, many moons passed, but no baby arrived. Joy spread throughout the village when Thundercloud and Dancing Star finally had a baby girl. She was beautiful with long hands and thick black hair. It took them three days to decide on her name.

Because they had waited so long for their baby, they named her Princess Running Late.

Johannes Spreen loved sports, especially track, tennis, and baseball. He pitched for the New York Police Department Baseball Team and participated in the NYPD bowling team. Here he holds the trophy for the 110th precinct bowling team in Queens who came in first place.

Spreen holds the NYPD 110th precinct bowling trophy.

Spreen directed the Confidential Investigations Unit, reporting directly to the Chief Inspector, also called Police Chief in many cities. In 1961, Johannes was also appointed as liaison officer between the Police and Department of Parks, where his knowledge of human relations led to his innovative motor scooter program, to be described later. He also received a commendation for jumping into the East River to rescue a drowning man.

In February of 1963, Johannes' boss, New York City Police Department Chief Inspector, was told that Spreen's father died, and kindly went to the funeral home to pay his respects. To the Chief Inspector's surprise, he found two bodies on view—Johannes's father *and* brother were both buried on the same day having died only one day apart. His cigar-maker father and brother were long-time smokers who died of lung cancer. Johannes mercifully withheld from his dying father that the son had just preceded him in death. His mother had died in 1957.

The sad newspaper notice of his father and brother's death in 1963 follows.

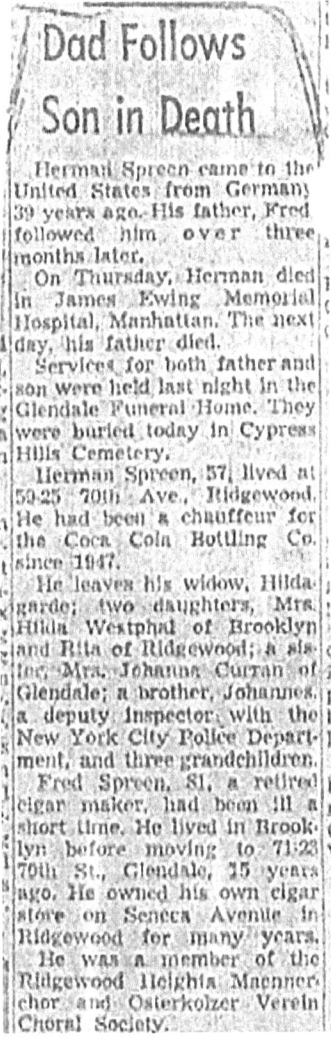

Dad Follows Son in Death

Herman Spreen came to the United States from Germany 39 years ago. His father, Fred, followed him over three months later.

On Thursday, Herman died in James Ewing Memorial Hospital, Manhattan. The next day, his father died.

Services for both father and son were held last night in the Glendale Funeral Home. They were buried today in Cypress Hills Cemetery.

Herman Spreen, 57, lived at 59-25 70th Ave., Ridgewood. He had been a chauffeur for the Coca Cola Bottling Co. since 1947.

He leaves his widow, Hildagarde; two daughters, Mrs. Hilda Westphal of Brooklyn and Rita of Ridgewood; a sister, Mrs. Johanna Curran of Glendale; a brother, Johannes, a deputy inspector with the New York City Police Department, and three grandchildren.

Fred Spreen, 81, a retired cigar maker, had been ill a short time. He lived in Brooklyn before moving to 71-23 70th St., Glendale, 15 years ago. He owned his own cigar store on Seneca Avenue in Ridgewood for many years.

He was a member of the Ridgewood Heights Maennerchor and Osterkolzer Verein Choral Society.

On February 4, 1963, the **Long Island Press** covered the death of Spreen's father and brother.

As he approached the climax of his career with NYPD in 1964, Spreen put nine experimental scooters into service in Manhattan's Central Park and Brooklyn's Prospect Park. Robbery and other crimes dropped significantly in the two parks during the four-month trial period.

Johannes recalled that one of his reserve police officers in the Parks Department was author Max Wylie, brother of Philip Wylie, also an author. Johannes tried to assist in solving the murders of Max Wylie's daughter and Emily Hoffert—the Career Girls Murder case that led to the Miranda decision and prohibition of execution in New York. Max Wylie wrote a book about the murders in 1964 called *Career Girl, Watch Your Step*. He invited Spreen and New York Mayor John Lindsay to his home to give Spreen a dedicated copy. Wylie wrote, "For Inspector Johannes Spreen. In appreciation for his fine service to this city and his support of the auxiliaries with the true respect of his friend, Sgt. Max Wylie. October 14, 1964."

Janice Wylie, *Newsweek* researcher (l) and schoolteacher Emily Hoffert were killed August 28, 1963.

Max Wylie at gun practice after his daughter was murdered.

A black man, 19-year-old George Whitmore, Jr., was first arrested for the murders. Later, Richard Robles, 22, a heroin user, confessed to the murders. An investigator who was depicted by Telly Savalas in a movie, (which led to the television series called *Kojak*) solved the case.

On June 13, 1966, the Supreme Court cited George Whitmore, Jr.'s, conviction as they issued the *Miranda* decision regarding the rights of criminal suspects. They wrote, "[T]he most conspicuous example occurred in New York in 1964, when an African American confessed to two brutal murders and a rape which he had not committed." Young Whitmore sued the New York City Police Department but without success.

Spreen's success with motor scooter cops created the introduction of more scooters. Spreen was pleased when Michael J. Murphy, New York City Police Commissioner in 1964 promoted his concept of scooters by saying, "…the rugged and versatile scooter opens new vistas in crime control. As its use grows it is anticipated that the 'scooter patrol' will provide unprecedented control over crime and criminals in all our far-flung recreational areas." It was later extended throughout the entire city.

Johannes received his master's degree from the College of Police Science of the City University in New York from the chancellor and the chairman of the Board of Education in a ceremony of changing hats pictured here.

NYPD Deputy Inspector Johannes Spreen changes hats
to receive his mortarboard and CUNY degree.

Shortly before Spreen's graduation, President John F. Kennedy was
assassinated on November 22, 1963. Jackie Kennedy and her children
generated publicity after Kennedy's assassination in 1963. After the assassination, Jackie tried to raise her children giving them educational,
physical, emotional, and spiritual values. Some of these translated into
taking them for adventures that their father would have provided. She
came with her little son nicknamed Jon-Jon born in 1960, to have a
ride on a scooter. Even though Spreen and the NYPD did not capture
a picture of little Jon-Jon riding on a scooter, this picture is an example
of what Jackie tried to do for her children when they no longer had a
father.

Jacqueline Kennedy and son sledding in 1965.

Spreen's Scooter Program continued and in September 1965, 50 more scooters were put into service in 17 precincts, still primarily for park patrol. Each precinct commander evaluated the experiment, reported favorably, and requested that the Scooter Program continue.

As his success with the scooter program grew, Johannes Spreen rose to Operations Inspector in 1965. During the visit of Pope Paul VI on October 4, 1965, the scooter patrolmen were invaluable to commanding officers along a motorcade route lined with over a million persons as shown in the this photograph. Scooter officers served as reconnaissance scouts, inter-sector messengers, and liaison officers when communications were severed or overtaxed.

Pope Paul in a Popemobile in New York, October 4, 1965.

Beginning October 20, 1965, Spreen had the Scooter Program tested for general street patrol in 15 selected precincts, and it was received favorably. An electrical power failure occurred November 9-10, 1965, during the height of an evening rush hour and several million persons were stalled in transit. However, the Scooter Patrol maintained immediate and direct radio communication with precinct station houses. A scooter was sent from Manhattan to Maspeth, Queens, over a jammed Williamsburg Bridge for emergency radio equipment, impossible for an auto, but it went and returned promptly.

The New York City Police Commissioner, Vincent L. Broderick, supported Spreen's Scooter Program in 1965 saying, "The scooter is the most effective police patrol technique which has been developed in recent years. It preserves the concept of the foot patrolman and yet provides a mobility and responsiveness which the foot patrolman lacks."

Commissioner Broderick changed his budget at the end of 1965 to include the purchase of 700 scooters for city street coverage after its surprising success. Inquiries came from many cities in the United States and foreign countries for information and specific operational techniques. The concept was really the progenitor of the community-oriented policing concept which was later to develop.

Spreen also found the Scooter Program to be effective during the paralyzing citywide transit strike January 1-13, 1966, when public transportation was nonexistent. Scooters were in constant demand because they could cut through traffic blockages, even driving on sidewalks when necessary. Besides quickly unlocking vehicular congestion, they could survey problem areas and report to precinct commanders. Near bridges and tunnels, when traffic lanes were reversed to expedite the flow of vehicles, the scooter officers were utilized most effectively. They also delivered messages and supplies through otherwise impassable locations.

Spreen's Scooter Program was also covered in the *New York Times* and the *New Yorker Magazine*, one of which is included in the appendix. By then scooter officers patrolled all New York City streets because captains in all 79 precincts liked them. Johannes' commented in one article, "We have got to win the hearts and minds of people, all people in the United States, and we need their assistance in the battle against crime and efforts to keep our communities safe and habitable. We must allow police to return to the people."

Spreen wrote an article for *The Journal of Criminal Law, Criminology and Police Science* published by Northwestern University in Volume 57, 1966, No. 3, p. 349-353. In those days, few police executives wrote articles for scholarly publications. His article was called "The Motor Scooter—An Answer to a Police Problem." Here is a summary.

A foot patrolman on a scooter easily covers at least five times the territory he could by walking a beat, and more efficiently. In a car, a patrolman's view is partly obstructed within the car. The scooter patrolman has 360 degrees visibility. The two-wheeled scooter is the ideal patrol vehicle to cut through traffic-clogged streets that block any three or four-wheeled vehicle. A scooter can be purchased for several hundred dollars, and uses less gas than a patrol car.

Constant foot patrol is fatiguing at best. The opportunity to ride as well as walk stimulates and quickens a man's job interest. A more active police officer has a greater sense of individual contribution to the police effort. A parked scooter patrolman draws youngsters like a magnet. The attraction has led to a new opportunity for the patrolman to establish rapport with the younger generation, which we hope will grow to adult respect as the youngsters mature, as well as an aid in recruiting.

The two-wheeled scooter can be operated safely if there is proper selection, screening, and training of manpower. That the scooter must be used as a slow moving protective patrol device and not as a high-speed pursuit vehicle must be inculcated in the minds of the patrolmen. We have found that three days of training suffices. During heavy rain or snow, the scooters are placed out of service.

For the cost of ten police officers for one year, a city can buy about 300 scooters. The anti-crime value of the 300 scooters weighed against the negligible effect of adding ten patrolmen to a large force tips the scale decidedly in favor of the scooters.

Spreen's Tactical Scooter Unit became a team patrol that kept in touch by radio. They operated either as partners or as a group according to the need. From this point on, the use of scooters became an accepted part of New York police operations, some 700 being acquired and put into operation by the time Spreen retired from the Department in 1966.

On March 17, 1966, Spreen and Mayor John Lindsay marched down Fifth Avenue for the Saint Patrick's Day parade. This was Lindsay's first appearance as mayor. The city had just endured a long subway strike. Now, it was in the midst of a hot battle over a civilian police-review board. The crowds had received Lindsay in cool silence. He was dubious about marching. However, Spreen and others assured him that all would go well. All along Fifth Avenue, the Mayor was greeted with tremendous cheering. Lindsay was beaming when he came to the reviewing stand, where city police and government officials gave him the usual Saint Patrick's Day greeting—"'May you be in heaven for twenty minutes before the Devil discovers that you're dead.'"

In a rather interesting return to the past, after many years of not using scooters that Spreen introduced, the New York Police Department began field testing four all-electric scooters in 2007. Their rational was that they offer police three attractive benefits: reduced fuel costs, lowered vehicle emissions, and, more practically, the element of surprise — the scooters' nearly-silent engines allow two-wheeled cops to approach suspects with more discretion.

Similar to scooters, another of Spreen's recommendations in his first book *(American Police Dilemma* in 2003*)* was Segways to be used by law enforcement officers trying to having closer communication with citizens while also moving quicker than an officer walking a beat. He was ahead of his time because then only two police departments were trying them out. Since then, many police departments now use Segways: Albuquerque, New Mexico; Glendale, New Hampshire; Greensboro, North Carolina; Auburn, Maine; Lakeland, Florida; Pittsfield, New Hampshire; Millford, Ohio; Surprise, Arizona; Iowa City, Iowa; Chesterfield, Missouri; Fond du Lac, Wisconsin; San Marcos, Texas; Savannah, Georgia; Cincinnati, Ohio; St. Paul, Minnesota; Richmond, Virginia; New Rochelle, New York; Atlanta, Georgia; Chicago, Illinois; Washington, D.C.; Lincoln, Nebraska; New York, NY; Philadelphia, Pennsylvania; and countless others.

Inspector Spreen and New York Mayor John Lindsay
walking down Fifth Avenue on St. Patrick's Day, 1966.

Spreen noted that in the 1950s and 60s as police became more modernized and motorized, crime still increased, community tensions exacerbated, and youth hostility rose. He believed these problems resulted from the police officer being set apart from people in his police car, dealing impersonally with the public and being less involved in neighborhood interactions. He compared our loss of respect for physicians who don't want to talk with us about our problems but simply write prescriptions and order things that affect our very lives.

"The good, trusted police officer of yesterday has now given way to the 'law enforcement officer' which implies a punitive or repressive role," said Spreen. Even today, he believes the bicycle, Segway or scooter can literally bring back the beat or foot patrol officer who interacts with the public.

Johannes found that in New York, "macho" cops looked with disdain at the two-wheeled vehicle. They preferred "hot" motorcycles. Yes, they were good for escorts and chasing speeders, as a "pursuit and punitive" machine, said Spreen, but t   he motor scooter is a "protective patrol vehicle."

Scooters, Spreen assured, would be cheaper to purchase, cheaper to supply with gas, and could be equipped with headlights, strobe lights, 50 pounds of equipment, and even sirens. They require a drivers' license and/or a motorcycle license.

The introduction and success of scooters was obvious to police officers in New York and elsewhere. It was recently praised on the New York police Website: The Squad Room on January 23, 2004, where the authors wrote about advances in policing:

> Expansion of Scooter Patrol: 1968
> In 1966, the department used scooter primarily in parks. In 1968, the department purchased over 200 more of these two-wheel scooters, and another 300 were added in 1969.
> The concept of scooter patrols in New York was made a reality through the efforts of a retired Inspector, Johannes Spreen, who later went on to become the Commissioner of the Detroit Police Department. It was the addition and expansion of police portable radio transceivers that assisted in broadening the use of scooters as a means of providing professional police services, and the mobility and responsiveness which foot patrol lacked. It was 1968 that each precinct was directed to establish motor scooter squads to perform duty on two tours, 8-4 and 4-12.

Although Spreen was ahead of the times in his community concepts of policing, he was disappointed in the political manipulations of the uniformed services. He proudly retired from the NYPD in 1966 and became a professor at John Jay College of Criminal Justice in New York.

Oh, how he loved teaching. He was so excited about giving new police candidates the history of policing and his special emphasis on the need to be close to the citizens. He won so many teaching awards at the new John Jay College, they almost had to retire some of them. He inspired students who continue to be in contact with him to this day.

Spreen was very big on crime prevention. He gave countless talks to the community, law enforcement groups, and wrote innumerable articles about the need to prevent crime, rather than just apprehend criminals after the fact.

He described how increasing crime rates produced increasing costs to citizens. There are more prosecutions, and more prosecutors to be educated and placed on the public payroll. As court loads increase, more trials generate the need for more courts and court personnel, including judges. Correction and punishment involve a greater investment in jails and prisons and their supervision. Probation needs escalate. The penalized criminal may have a family whose support then becomes a social welfare burden.

Worst of all, Spreen commented, what happens to the image of a community when crime and disorder spreads? How do you measure the loss to the community when its best and most prosperous citizens flee from the danger, discomfort and unpleasantness of community crime, never to return? How do you measure the flight of business and industry, the shoppers who no longer come to the community to shop, the meetings, conventions and tourists that no longer use its facilities?

That was Spreen's pitch in police work and at John Jay and everybody knew it. Because of that pitch, he was to be the new Commissioner of the Detroit Police Department. Here was the chance to put into action all the things he had believed and taught for so many years.

CHAPTER THREE:
Spreen Learned of Detroit's History

Johannes Spreen soon found that Detroit was unlike any other American city and would present new and different problems. He looked deeply into the history of the troubled city to try to create solutions for its problems. Having started the successful motor scooter program in New York City, he was interested to learn that in 1897, Detroit police began use of bicycles. The first bicycle patrol officers were known as "scorchers." The scorchers were expert bicyclists employed for the express purpose of apprehending other speeding bicyclists.

Police cars replaced this in about 1909. One amazing picture of a police car shows an officer standing in the back seat, Burton Girardin, grandfather of Ray Girardin, the police commissioner whom Johannes replaced.

Spreen was an excellent researcher. He soon learned that Stalin had sent Communism to Detroit. In 1922, Stalin approved of spending $300,000 to spread communist propaganda among blacks. In 1925, 12 Detroit blacks were selected to be trained in Russia. Delighted to find receptive ears among black workers, in 1928 Stalin sent Hungarian communist leader Joseph Pogany (alias John Pepper, John Schwartz, John Swift, etc.) to America to set blacks against whites. Pogany was to stir blacks up with the desire to create their own republic within America.

This was not an entirely new idea. Many blacks in the South were lured by pamphlets to Oklahoma after the Civil War. The pamphlets dangled the promise of setting it up as the first completely black state. Eventually 27 black towns grew to encompass 10 percent of the Indian Territory's population by the time Oklahoma joined the union in 1907.

Stalin's goal, of course, was that racial hegemony would increase the number of communists, and disrupt the American government. In 1928, Pogany distributed a pamphlet to blacks for the Communist Party of the United States of America (CPUSA) called *American Negro Problems: A Program of Racial Strife for the United States.*

The pamphlet urged blacks to use violence if necessary in their struggle for national self-determination. It suggested propaganda to smear the emerging black middle class with terms such as "Uncle Toms" and agents of the "white capitalist". Its proposal to establish a black separate government within the U.S. stated, "Self-determination means the right to establish their own state, to erect their own government, if they choose to do so… The Negro Communists should emphasize in their propaganda the establishment of a Negro Soviet Republic."

By 1928, Henry Ford's assembly line and fame in car production put Detroit on the world map. Pogany had found that blacks and other workers felt oppressed by capitalist bosses. However, he also knew of the superior technology in the automotive industry. Therefore, Stalin sent a group of Russians to meet with Ford in Detroit. Stalin wanted Ford's help to establish a Russian car manufacturing company to make the Model A.

A contract was signed between Henry's son, Edsel Ford, and the Russians to build two plants, one in Novgorod and the other in Moscow. Russians were sent to Detroit to learn the automotive industry and Americans were sent to Russia to build the plants and assemble some 70,000 cars and trucks.

The construction of "Soviet Detroit" in Novgorod and Moscow by Ford's engineers and workers became bogged down by Russian ineptitude. By 1932, Stalin broke the contracts and placed orders for cars in Europe and Russia, rather than America.

Even before the beginning of this strong communist influence in Detroit, American blacks as well as whites had a great attraction to the promises of the communist party for the lowly worker, oppressed by big business capitalists.

Despite the Great Depression, Mexican painter Diego Rivera, a life-long Marxist, was invited by Henry Ford to paint the famous murals on the walls of the Detroit Institute of Art. Rivera's work depicted industrial life in the United States and concentrated on the car plant workers of Detroit. From April 1932 to March 1933 Diego painted, accompanied by his wife, artist Frida Kahlo. Diego visited workers' homes, neighborhoods, salt mines, railroad cars, chemical plants, blast furnaces and the Ford Rouge plant to paint his murals. He found racial diversity and depicted the "yellow, red, black and white" races in his paintings.

His politics and therefore his art were criticized later but Edsel Ford defended the work. Rivera's paintings provided the first inspiration for Franklin Roosevelt's Works Projects Administration (WPA) program in later years.

Detroit Industry, South Wall by Diego Rivera, 1932–33

Spreen learned that the communist influence lingered in the Detroit automotive plants, and especially in the labor unions. Coleman Young, a later political critic of Spreen, was influenced early on by communism. He later became Detroit's first black mayor from 1974-1993, after Spreen finished his post as police commissioner. However, in those early days, Young was fired by Ford Motor Company for his union activities during the 1930s. United Auto Workers (UAW) employee Walter Reuther urged the union to dismiss those with communist leanings, and Young was ejected.

Young was called before the House Un-American Activities Committee (HUAAC) in 1952, and interrogated regarding his ties to the Communist Party. He accused the Committee of being "un-American" because they were not doing more for the voting rights of blacks living in the South. He said that if it was communistic to defend the rights of workers, then he was a communist. The account of his interrogation helped build his reputation as a forceful union and civil rights organizer. Young ran for the Detroit Common Council in 1960. In 1961, he won election as a delegate to the state senate, where he served as floor leader for the Democrats in 1966.

Before all that, Walter Reuther, himself, was let go by Detroit's Ford Company because of his union activities in 1933. Reuther traveled with his brother to Russia where he worked in the Molotov Auto Works in Novgorod for two years in an *unheated* plant. After learning of working conditions in Russia, Reuther went on to China and then Japan to see working conditions there. When he returned in 1935, he was reinstated in Detroit union activities where he soon led the UAW, and became thoroughly anti-Soviet!

Another person in Walter Reuther's UAW was John Conyers, Sr., father of John and Nathan Conyers who both are still active in the car dealership business and politics in Detroit today. The elder Conyers led strikes for equal wages with whites in the 1930s and 1940s. John Conyers, Jr. and Spreen would have their run-ins in the late 1960s.

The next thing that Johannes Spreen learned was that Detroit was the birthplace of Muslim movements. The Nation of Islam (NOI) was one of the many truly unusual organizations that was to create problems for law enforcement during Spreen's term and thereafter. W. D. Fard in Detroit organized the Nation of Islam about 1933. Fard claimed to be from Mecca or Arabia, but may have been from California. He arrived in 1930 as a door-to-door silk clothing salesman, who told black customers of their national origins and stressed the supremacy of blacks over whites. He came to the attention of Elijah Poole, who later renamed himself Elijah Muhammad.

When young, Elijah Poole moved to Detroit in search of work, and worked six years in the Chevrolet auto plant. He joined the Universal Negro Improvement Association (UNIA), an organization created to instill black pride. Some Detroit blacks ran into trouble with the law because they objected to the draft, claiming their ancestors were brought to America against their will and they shouldn't be drafted. Elijah was arrested May 8, 1942, for failing to register for the draft. While in prison for evading the draft, he taught classes on the doctrines of the NOI. He was released in 1946, and was appointed as Chief Minister of Islam in the NOI order. When he died in 1975, his place was taken over by Louis Farrakhan who is active to this day. These groups were to cause much consternation for the Detroit Police Department.

Spreen learned how the unions created black-white friction. With easy access to iron resources and good railroad transportation, Detroit was the perfect setting for the automotive industry. Henry Ford's generous wages, assembly line and management style kept union membership low until the outset of World War II, when unions began to increase membership.

The unions were damned if they did include blacks and damned if they didn't. They wanted members, but whites didn't want blacks to be part of the union, and certainly not part of its leadership. So the UAW made a show of including blacks, but since black members knew they had little say in the union, tension was high.

During the war, the automobile industry shifted to manufacturing military equipment and war machinery. Detroit was transformed into an "Arsenal of Democracy". Recruiters toured the south, convincing whites and blacks to head for Detroit war factories and high wages. Workers responded and streamed into Detroit, which had not sufficiently planned how to handle all the newcomers.

The influx strained housing, transportation, education and recreation facilities. Men and women, black and white, including a variety of other ethnic groups, worked at breakneck speed to provide American military forces with their requirements.

Stalin would later say that Germany was "defeated by Detroit." Russia, as an ally of the U.S. during World War II, benefited from Detroit directly. Their Red Army tanks as well as American tanks were products of Detroit's technology.

The war years of 1941-45 created disequilibrium as blacks rushed in to fill "white jobs". Whites feared competition for their jobs and objected to housing integration. Thus, despite decent wages, blacks were constrained to live in deteriorating houses, segregated from whites, often without indoor plumbing.

Not only did whites object to living near blacks, but they also protested working with them. In June 1943, about 25,000 Packard plant workers stopped work to demonstrate against the promotion of three blacks. The strikers shouted, "I'd rather see Hitler and Hirohito win than work beside a nigger on the assembly line."

Women workers tried unsuccessfully to get men to walk off the job to show disapproval of black female workers using the white restrooms. "They think their fannies are as good as ours," screamed one woman.

The Ku Klux Klan wearing white hoods and the Black Legion with black hoods and weapons actively harassed minorities in this hateful Detroit atmosphere. The Black Legion was militantly trying to keep foreigners, blacks and communists out of factories. Humphrey Bogart starred in the 1937 movie *Black Legion* about this destructive group with Detroit origins.

The black surge into Detroit during the war brought another figure to prominence—George Crockett, Jr. He was the first black lawyer in the U.S. Department of Labor in the 1930s and then made a name for himself as head of the UAW's Fair Practices Committee where he tried to root out auto factory racism. However, when Walter Reuther emerged as president of the union, he replaced Crockett.

After being ousted from the UAW, George Crockett helped found Detroit's first integrated law firm. He defended a black man accused of being a communist. Crockett and four other lawyers were sentenced to prison for four months for defending one of 11 people charged in the Smith Act trial in New York in 1949 and 1950. During this viral anti-communist McCarthy era, being a communist sympathizer was deemed as bad as being a card carrying communist or plotting to overthrow the U.S. government.

Spreen would interact with Crockett on the worst day of his administration when Crockett released suspects who were arrested in the murder at the New Bethel Church.

Spreen also learned of Detroit's new breed of religious and government representatives. In the late 1940s, the charismatic Rev. Clarence LeVaughn Franklin (C. L. Franklin was the father of Aretha Franklin) moved to Detroit to found New Bethel Baptist Church. Franklin had a very distinctive preaching style, so unique that tapes and CDs of his sermons were used to train preachers. In the 1950s, he preached accompanied by a group of gospel singers, including Aretha who went on to become a well-known singer.

In post-war America, the desire to own a home and a car, the development of Detroit's freeway system in 1950, and low gas prices drove the automotive economy to new heights. The big three giants in the car industry, Chrysler, Ford and General Motors, all developed in Detroit. High wages and the proliferation of unions, especially the United Automotive Workers (UAW), drove wages and benefits even higher. The results of black migration from the South for unskilled jobs and high wages in the automotive industry swelled Detroit's black population to 16.4%. In the mid-1950s, Detroit's population climaxed with just over 1.8 million and has declined ever since.

In 1953, Congregational minister Albert Cleage, Jr., and a group of followers left the United Church of Christ to found the Central Congregation Church. He grew up in Detroit, earned his B.A. from Wayne State University, and his Bachelor of Divinity from Oberlin Graduate School of Theology. This pastor denounced traditional leadership. He claimed the "Uncle toms" who buttered up white bosses betrayed black Detroit. This set blacks against blacks and stirred further the pot of hatred in the city.

In 1957, the Detroit Branch of the NAACP issued a report on police brutality entitled: *Analysis of Police Brutality Complaints Reported to the Detroit Branch of the National Association for the Advancement of Colored People in the Period from January 1, 1956 to July 30, 1957.* It brought about changes under the next police commissioner, Herbert Hart. In 1959, Hart initiated integrated patrol cars in Detroit.

Housing problems developed when blacks wanted to live near their work, but whites refused to accept mixed neighborhoods. So blacks moved into downtown Detroit. That precipitated white flight to the suburbs. The real estate profession, housing authorities in Detroit and the Common Council shared the blame for maintaining extreme segregation in housing.

In addition, an influx of unskilled blacks into a community of unskilled whites evoked extremely strong reactions. Whites feared that their jobs and income might be in jeopardy. These reactions set whites against blacks. In 1960, the population of Detroit was beginning to shrink, and by then 29% of the city was black.

Rev. Cleage and Rev. C. L. Franklin not only preached but also held organizational meetings of black power groups at the New Bethel church in 1963. The groups included the NAACP, Group for the Advancement of Leadership, UHURU (founded by Wayne State students), Detroit chapter of the Student Non-Violent Coordinating Committee, and the Revolutionary Action Movement (RAM). Cleage added to his prominence in 1967 when he developed a novel approach to reverse black oppression. Cleage zealously preached of a black Madonna, and established the Shrine of the Black Madonna for a black woman who gave birth to a black baby Jesus.

Cleage and Franklin caused Spreen and Detroit law enforcement officers no end of problems because they supported arming militant blacks.

John Conyers, Sr., who had worked for the UAW to bring equal wages for blacks and whites, campaigned for the ouster of Detroit Mayor Louis Miriani because the white mayor was openly critical of blacks. Shortly before Spreen went to Detroit, Jerome Cavanagh defeated Miriani who then served on the City Council during Spreen's term as Commissioner. He and Spreen often differed over law enforcement issues.

Spreen became police commissioner shortly after Detroit began to lose automotive jobs. Heedless of small, well-built fuel-efficient foreign cars, Detroit carmakers paid little attention to competition until it was too late. With careless disregard for quality or fuel efficiency, new gas-guzzlers with minor aesthetic changes debuted each year.

Greedy car companies participated in the economic demise of Detroit when they began to outsource work to areas with lower wages to maintain their profits. They appeared unconcerned that many people had moved into Detroit to work for them. Car manufacturers moved some plants to suburbs and other areas, leaving unemployed blacks in the center of the city, surrounded by closed, vacant and burned out buildings. Detroit was ripe for the major U.S. riot of the 1960s.

Various splinter groups of socialist and communist persuasion were welcome among the working class of Detroit. Some Detroiters and members of the Socialist Workers Party joined the Fair Play for Cuba Committee (made famous by Lee Harvey Oswald in 1963) and visited Cuba.

Spreen found that the emergence of black militants in Detroit was linked to a former Detroit worker who went to Cuba. Robert Williams, who would become a hero among black nationalists during Spreen's administration, had worked at the Ford Motor Plant in Detroit from 1942 to 1944, when he was drafted into the Army. Upon discharge, Williams led a group of 40 armed blacks to oppose a parade of the Ku Klux Klan who intended to display the dead body of a black veteran. Not a shot was fired but Williams became convinced that armed self-defense of blacks was necessary.

Williams went to college, rejoined the military (Marines) and after an early discharge because of his agitation, became a leader of the local NAACP branch. When he was accused of a kidnapping, he fled to Cuba. Robert Williams supported the Cuban Revolution. Communists and Fidel Castro welcomed him in 1961. In Cuba, he ran Radio Free Dixie. While there, he wrote *Negroes with Guns* in 1962 about the need for blacks to defend themselves with arms against the Ku Klux Klan and the white police forces. After a falling out with Cuban leaders, dodging arrest in the United States, he went to China where Mao's communists welcomed him. He was there when he was named the first president of the Republic of New Africa (RNA). This militant group which originated in Detroit became a major obstacle for Spreen's administration with the New Bethel Church shootout, to be described later.

Robert Williams (l) with Red China's Chairman Mao Tse-tung (r).

Detroit attorney Milton Henry and his brothers organized yet another black movement. Milton was given a dishonorable discharge from the military because he complained about the segregation of black officers. After completing Yale Law School, he became an attorney. Milton and his two brothers, Lawrence and Richard, met with Malcolm X. The Henry brothers established a Detroit group called Group on Advanced Leadership (GOAL) and invited Malcolm X to speak. He delivered his famous "Message to the Grassroots" speech just before President John Kennedy's assassination in November 1963. Some 700-800 mostly black workers attended. Malcolm X expounded on his support for the Cuban revolution, the Chinese revolution, and opposition to the "rulers" in this country.

Detroit attorney, Milton Henry, and Malcolm X in Detroit.

In 1964, Rev. Franklin came up with a huge media event to increase the intensity of civil rights and black freedom in Detroit. Franklin invited Rev. Martin Luther King, Jr., to Detroit for a "Walk to Freedom" on June 23, 1964. Rev. Franklin, Rev. King, Walter Reuther and Mayor Cavanagh led the march, which was followed by King's "I Have a Dream" speech (*I Have a Dream: Writings,* 1992).

Rev. M. L. King, Jr., (far left) and Walter Reuther, (far right) and others lead Detroit's "Walk to Freedom" on June 23, 1964.

In March 1965, the Citizens' Committee for Equal Opportunity (CCEO) worried that Detroit blacks might follow some of these "less responsible" black leaders. There was heightened racial consciousness and group movements to increase racial pride. Black demands were made on white leaders and ferment in the black community ensued.

Meanwhile, John Conyers, Jr., became a lawyer. He was moving up in visibility and influence. He was elected to Congress in 1965, where he still serves. He became a frequent agitator on the Detroit scene complaining of police repression and brutality.

In 1966, George Crockett won a seat on the Recorder's Court in Detroit. He began to criticize judges and lawyers for perpetrating the American doctrine of racism and said that whites used the law as a "handmaiden of the propertied class" to repress blacks.

Black extremists said successful black middle class were "Oreos," black on the outside, white on the inside. Blacks were at odds with each other. Many claimed the city administrators; NAACP and Detroit Urban League cared nothing about those in the slums. Thus, those black groups were among those responsible for the "spontaneous protests" and other actions that sparked the 1967 riot.

Commissioner Spreen's black friend, Hubert Locke, attached to Police Commissioner Girardin's office under Mayor Cavanagh's administration wrote *The Detroit Riot of 1967*. He portrayed the racial dilemmas in big cities. He said it was immaterial whether black men or white men made decisions because it was like arguing over who will be on the bridge or at the helm when the ship sinks.

Rev. Albert Cleage again created headlines when he launched the Black Christian National Movement in Detroit in 1967. Cleage rejected integration and stressed self-determination and black separatism. He advocated that blacks should think black, vote black, and buy black if they were to be free. Cleage urged blacks to defend themselves against brutality and strike back when knocked down. He called for black churches to reinterpret Jesus' teachings to suit the needs of black people. On Easter Sunday of 1967, he unveiled an 18-foot painting of a Black Madonna and renamed his church the Shrine of the Black Madonna.

Black Madonna and Baby Jesus at the Shrine of the Black Madonna.

Elijah Muhammad called Christianity the "white man's religion" to pacify blacks by keeping them focused on heavenly rewards, but Cleage wanted Christianity to be valuable to blacks so he blackened Jesus. After the 1967 riots, he published *The Black Messiah*, which rendered his version of Jesus as a black revolutionary leader.

After the riot of July 1967, Cleage led a memorial service for those killed. Mayor Cavanagh and Governor Romney attended. Rev. Cleage declared, "We are engaged in a nation-wide rebellion, seeking to become what God intended that we should be—free men with control of our own destiny, the destiny of black men." (Widick, 189).

When Commissioner Spreen arrived, he learned of the FBI and police surveillance of black groups and radical organizations that advocated bearing arms. He also found that FBI and police surveillance was used to gain information about Michigan State University students who planned a rally to support integrated housing.

Spreen expected that New Detroit, Inc., which began as a temporary committee of concerned citizens after the riots, would be helpful. After the riot, Gov. George Romney and Mayor Cavanagh called 150 local leaders to help return order to the city. They were asked to donate the services of several high-ranking managers and specialists. The heads of Ford, General Motors and Chrysler, the UAW, three major banks and three utilities met with community leaders and activists to discuss Detroit's problems. A coalition with a pledged budget of $3.5 million called New Detroit, Inc. emerged.

New Detroit incorporated, expanded, and eventually obtained as much as $10 million a year from major businesses in Detroit. They helped disadvantaged and minority groups in housing, education, employment, community services, recreation, etc. A staff and volunteers from private industry (paid by their employers for their time) operated new Detroit. The board of trustees welcomed ADC mothers, including black ghetto militants, and neighborhood improvement leaders to discuss problems with the city leaders, including major auto company executives.

New Detroit, Inc. worked hard to understand why people rioted. One early finding was that 100,000+ housing units in Detroit in 1968 were substandard. Many apartments affordable by blacks had poor plumbing, no locks, cracked windows, peeling paint and unsafe stairways. With rampant unemployment, poverty and crime, New Detroit operated much like a social agency. Meetings were long and emotional, but New Detroit was unable to keep whites from leaving and to keep jobs from vanishing.

Joe Hudson, whose family was intertwined with the Hudson Motor Car Company, was a good example of the problem in Detroit. Hudson's corporate policy was to open additional department stores in the suburbs, pulling residents out of the city to shop. Thus, Hudson and others had contributed to the economic decline of the inner city. His department stores finally merged with Fields.

Another early head of New Detroit Inc. was Max Fisher. The son of poor Russian Jewish immigrants, he got into oil and spread out with investments, including malls on the outskirts of Detroit. He was a financial supporter of Richard Nixon and Gerald Ford. He helped the Renaissance Center, the United Fund drive and the Detroit Symphony expansion. However, when Spreen came, Fisher was 60, thought of himself as a mover and shaker, and was no longer modest. Fisher never met with new Police Commissioner Spreen. Another founding member of New Detroit was Damon Keith, whom Spreen much admired.

These and other powerful personalities felt they knew best what Detroit needed as they pulled the strings of New Detroit, Inc. Although they wanted to play a major part in the recovery of the city, Spreen often found them working against the good of the city, favoring those who appeared before them.

One man eager to speak to New Detroit was a black militant named Frank Ditto. This street gang leader had written newsletters urging that police officers should be killed. However, he still got $250,000 from New Detroit for bogus reasons. Detroit businessmen visited Ditto's "Voice of Independence" headquarters shortly after the riots. Such radicals who had no good works to propose sopped up much of the money of New Detroit before Spreen arrived and continued during his term.

A group called TransLove which advocated free love, marijuana decriminalization, and the end of war in Vietnam had promoted a Love-In on Belle Isle on April 30, 1967, some 2 ½ months before the Detroit riot. Only a few mounted police appeared because the group had promised a peaceful gathering. The crowd of 6,000 became rowdy after imbibing beer, wine and drugs. As some tried to light bonfires with trash, a man driving a motorcycle wildly through the crowd was arrested. Someone threw a firecracker toward the police horses, and soon rocks and bottles were thrown as well as more firecrackers. More police were summoned. Then they formed a line and slowly moved the crowd onto the bridge and off the island. Windows were smashed, and businesses began to close down. Police attacked spectators and news photographers when they photographed some beatings. TransLove was still active in Detroit by the time Spreen arrived.

Another group began to form just before Johannes arrived in Detroit. Some of those who formed the Black Panther Party in 1966 in Chicago came to Detroit to assist the fledgling black communist group called the Revolutionary Action Movement (RAM). The Detroit RAM group was later renamed Detroit Revolutionary Union Movement (DRUM) when blacks took over including former Wayne State University students.

A number of "hate groups" proliferated and the FBI had initiated a program called COINTELPRO to discredit and disorganize them. The FBI Special Agent in Charge of Detroit from February 1965 to May 1970 was Paul Stoddard, with whom Spreen had various dealings and communication. Spreen, however, was unaware of the insidious surveillance and disruption techniques used by the FBI under Hoover's administration.

On March 30-31, 1968, the Malcolm X Society held a national convention in Detroit to set up a black government called the Republic of New Africa (RNA). The conference was at the Shrine of the Black Madonna where Rev. Albert Cleage was pastor. The Malcolm X Society promoted various Black Nationalist activities. They used this name because Malcolm Little, slain black leader, was known as an advocate of Black Power.

A black Detroit police lieutenant was working undercover when black nationalists held a conference about separating from America to form the new government of the Republic of New Africa. Black lawyers, scientists, economists and industrialists met to speak to approximately 2,000 to 3,000 people. One speaker stated that the goal was to have a militia of both male and females, to be comprised of "twenty two million trigger fingers". Another spoke of the role of the black man in his attempt to deal with "the beast" (the United States). He said,

"This country must be brought to its knees and it will not be done by hope and sympathy." A proposal was made to aid blacks by forming black guerillas and the proposal was sent to the committee for study. Another proposal was made and adopted that black draft dodgers and black G.I.s who refused duty in Vietnam should be supported by the group and their attorneys.

Those present signed a Declaration of Independence from the United States. A leader announced that the delegates had named their new government the Republic of New Africa. Another speaker stressed that under the RNA black children would no longer be taught by white teachers and brainwashed with white doctrines. She claimed that the government was planning to get rid of black people, were starving Negro babies, drafting husbands and sons, and taking away poverty programs. She pointed out that the Vietnamese lured G.I.s into traps with sniper fire. She revealed that she *had used lure tactics to lead riot control police forces into ambush in Detroit.*

It had been suspected that during the 1967 Detroit riot, that blacks lured police and firemen into ambushes so that snipers could fire at them. Such a scenario may have occurred at the Algiers Motel.

Another speaker said that the new RNA nation would adopt African attire, African names, have their own holidays and heroes, and their great leaders like Malcolm X, all of which would be part of the "Voodoo". Then a long-time card-carrying member of the Communist Party (CPUSA) spoke next and attacked the courts as being biased and railroading thousands of Negroes to their deaths.

Malcolm X (Little's) widow advocated using weapons. She warned that when the whites get informers, they don't protect the informer once they are through with him.

Black Detroiter Richard Henry (Imari Obadele) came up with the idea of reparations for the RNA. The United States was to cede the contiguous states of Louisiana, Mississippi, Alabama, Georgia and South Carolina, to the blacks and pay $400 billion in reparations for the injustices done to black Americans during the slavery and segregation periods. After all, reparations were paid to Japanese Americans interned during WWII, and to American Indian tribes for their lands stolen by the government, they argued. The current reparation movement took form in 1988, when Richard Henry and his associates formed the National Coalition of Blacks for Reparations in America (N'COBRA.)

The RNA manifesto demanded a vote among African Americans to determine whether they wanted to form an independent nation within the United States. If it passed, the five contiguous states would then form an independent black nation. Individual blacks would get part of each government payment and the remainder would go to purchase land for the new republic.

The idea of creating several all black states with a vote was the topic of a book written by the spouse of author Holloway. *Tragedy in Black and White* by Bob Cheney was published in 2001 but was begun in 1970 when the RNA was promoting these ideas. The book depicts a fictional story of what might happen if such states were created and reparations demanded.

The RNA advocated community self-sufficiency, political rights, freedom of the press, banning of trade unions, mandatory military service, and the legalization of polygamy (practiced by some African tribes.)

The FBI considered the militant Republic of New Africa to be dangerous. They conducted raids, covert and overt repressive campaigns, and tried to disrupt them. The Detroit Police Department used surveillance and undercover officers to track their activities and tried to prevent violence.

Shortly after that first RNA meeting, a white man assassinated Rev. Martin Luther King, Jr., on April 4, 1968. Detroit blacks felt a special closeness since the visit when he began his "I Have a Dream" theme there. A walkout of black students at Detroit Cooley High School began walkouts from twenty other Detroit schools as well as walkouts by black workers at the Chrysler Jefferson Avenue Plant.

Activities in the automotive industry made news on May 2, 1968. A walkout of 4,000 workers at the Hamtramck Assembly Plant occurred because workers objected to an exhausting speed-up of the production line. This strike gave auto executives the chance to discharge black workers connected with DRUM, whom they perceived as the greatest agitators. Those discharges were covered in the third issue of the DRUM's newspaper. That issue attacked the UAW for endorsing the annual Detroit Police field day, and listed a number of deaths attributed to the police department.

The day after the walkout at Hamtramck, a rally for Rev. King was to be held at Cobo Hall, Detroit's Convention Center, on May 3rd. The rally, which was telecast over a local channel, was peaceful and orderly until a car stalled. At that point, the police and agitators became extremely aggressive, and 19 people were seriously injured. Black and liberal spokesmen denounced the actions of the police.

Robert Kennedy was scheduled to appear in Detroit two weeks later on May 15, 1968. It was expected to draw many listeners and agitators. However, a newspaper strike kept events in Detroit from drawing large crowds. The media strike lasted from November 16, 1967 until August 8, 1968, just after Spreen arrived to take his job in Detroit. Kennedy came to Detroit campaigning for the Presidency and speaking about Vietnam. At noon, when he arrived at Kennedy Square named for his brother, the throng was just about unmanageable. Following his speech, the crowd surged forward, lifted him up and carried him to his car, but no unseemly accidents occurred. Sadly, Robert Kennedy was assassinated three weeks later.

On May 29, 1968, Milton Henry (Brother Gaidi) as First Vice President of the Republic of New Africa wrote the following letter to Dean Rusk, Secretary of State. Richard Henry (Brother Imari) drove to Washington, D.C., and delivered it to the Department of State, handing it over to security guards outside the building.

Greetings:

This note is to advise you of the willingness of the Republic of New Africa to enter immediately into negotiations with the United States of America for the purpose of settling the long-standing grievances between our two peoples and correcting long-standing wrongs.

The wrongs to which we refer are those, of course, which attended the slavery of black people in this country and the oppression of black people, since slavery, which continues to our own day. The grievances relate to the failure of the United States to enter into any bilateral agreements with black people, either before or after the Civil War, which reflect free consent and true mutuality. Black people weren't given the choices of free people once the United States had ceased, theoretically, its enslavement of black people, and this constitutes a fatal defect in the attempt to impose U.S. citizenship upon blacks in America.

The existence of the Republic of New Africa poses a realistic settlement for these grievances and wrongs. We offer new hope for your country as for ours. We wish to see an end to war in the streets. We wish to lift from your country, from your people, the poorest, most depressed segment of the population, and, with them, work out our own destiny, on what has been the poorest states in your union (Mississippi, Louisiana, Alabama, Georgia, and South Carolina), making a separate, free, and independent black nation.

Our discussions should involve land and all those questions connected with the prompt transfer of sovereignty in black areas from the United States to the Republic of New Africa. They must also involve reparations. We suggest that a settlement of not less than $10,000 per black person be accepted as a basis for discussions. We do assure you that the Republic of New Africa remains ready instantly to open good faith negotiations, at a time and under conditions to be mutually agreed. We urge your acceptance of this invitation for talks in the name of peace, justice, and decency.

For the Republic,
Milton Henry

On May 30-June 1, 1968, the RNA met in Chicago. The speakers described the "birth" of the RNA, read the letter to Dean Rusk, described the 3% income tax for the new nation of RNA, established the military arm of the RNA, and set out objectives. Those objectives included an income tax; certificates for $100,000 to buy land in Mississippi, a savings stamp program; fundraising functions in this country and abroad; a cultural magazine; a theatrical group; a government printing office in Los Angeles; a national news magazine; and plans for literature to support votes and recruitment of citizens.

In June 1968, State Senator Coleman Young told the *Michigan Chronicle*, "If the Mayor is afraid to take on the DPOA (Detroit Police Officers Association) then we will do it for him. Otherwise this city is headed for a bloodbath."

On June 3, RNA representatives left Detroit for Tanzania, Africa, to confer with Robert Williams to secure financial help for the RNA from "Red China." During that meeting, Williams stated that he did not intend to make any statement or do anything on behalf of the RNA. He stated that he had no funds for the RNA and had expected them to bring funds to him to establish a hospital in Tanzania.

The Henrys returned on June 10, 1968, and held a cabinet. The lack of interest in the RNA and the intentions of Williams were announced to those who attended. This caused great consternation among members and they decided that if this were to reach the members, the RNA would probably fail. Williams did tell the Henrys to push for reparations and to obtain a large number of signatures to show the United States that the RNA had a large following.

On June 29, 1968, Richard Henry announced a petition drive to the members of the Detroit caucus of the RNA. The Detroit caucus was to obtain 30,000 signatures by August 8, 1968, and the petition was then to be presented to the United Nations. The petition insisted that the RNA be recognized as a "free black government" empowered to negotiate for reparations.

In late July just as Spreen arrived in Detroit, copies of the petition were mailed to RNA consulates in Ohio, New York and California with instructions to obtain 50,000 signatures by August 18, 1968. The placard had a picture of a smiling black couple and read:

WE ARE ASKING YOU TO VOTE FOR LAND AND POWER
Black people from all over America in convention in Detroit established the Republic of New Africa on 31 March 1968. We are working to build a separate free, powerful, rich, humane black nation on land reclaimed by black people in the South. All black people in America are eligible to become citizens and participate in election of officers to be held by January 1970.

We, the black people, in America, insist that the United States government and the world recognize our right to reparations—payment—from the United States government for the labor stolen from our ancestors during a century of slavery and for the damages suffered by all of us since slavery by reason of racial discrimination. We insist that the Republic of New Africa be recognized as the free black government empowered to negotiate for these reparations.

FOR EVERY PERSON: $10,000, $4,000 FOR THE INDIVIDUAL, $6,000 FOR THE REPUBLIC.

We, the undersigned black people in America, insist that the United States government and the world recognize our right to reparations—payment—from the United States government for the labor stolen from our ancestors during slavery and for the damages suffered by all of us since slavery, by reason of racial discrimination. We insist that the Republic of New Africa be recognized as the free black government empowered to negotiate for these reparations.

With all this going on, how did Detroit come to be called "A Model City?" It came about during Mayor Jerome P. Cavanagh's administration. During the previous decade, over 100,000 jobs had been lost as auto manufacturers such as Hudson, Studebaker and Packard closed. Cavanagh came into office with an unemployment rate of a staggering 18% in the black community, a huge city deficit, and a nearly all white police force which antagonized and degraded blacks with a constant "stop and frisk" mentality.

During Cavanagh's administration, the economy improved thanks to jobs provided by the big three auto manufacturers. The good years of 1962 to 1967 stimulated employment with the help of business and labor leaders. Detroit had a fairly large and prosperous black middle class. Blacks who worked in the automobile plants were paid 20% more than unskilled workers elsewhere in the nation were. Cavanagh, a likable young Irishman, handled his slate of problems with aplomb.

First, he hired a black city comptroller, Alfred Pelham. Several blacks were appointed to fill other important city posts. Then he appointed Michigan Supreme Court Judge George Edwards as police commissioner to reform the 4,000-man police department. Edwards served nearly two years (1962-63), attempted to increase the number of blacks in the department.

Mayor Cavanagh improved the poor financial position of Detroit by securing approval of an income tax of one percent for city residents and a half percent for non-residents who worked in the city. This greatly helped to put Detroit's finances in balance. The astute new mayor and his team strongly pursued federal aid to add to the city's tax base.

Between July 1, 1962 and August 1, 1967, Detroit received $230,422,000 from the federal government for one program or another. Cavanagh supported the Detroit NAACP (the largest branch in the nation) goals to ban housing discrimination, with members such as Rev. C. L. Franklin, Rev. Albert Cleage and politician John Conyers, Jr.

When Rev. Martin Luther King came to Detroit on June 23, 1963, Cavanagh was there with 125,000 to greet King and support the black freedom march and civil rights movement. It was the largest civil rights march in the nation up to that time. King delivered a speech that began,

> I have a dream this afternoon that one day right here in Detroit, Negroes will be able to buy a house or rent a house anywhere that their money will carry them; they will be able to get a job...
>
> I have a dream this evening that one day, we will recognize the words of Jefferson that all men are created equal—that they are endowed by their creator with certain inalienable rights, that among these are life, liberty and the pursuit of happiness...
>
> I have a dream this afternoon that the brotherhood of man will become a reality in this day, with this faith. I will go out and carve a tunnel of hope through the mountain of despair with this faith. I will go out with you and transform dark yesterdays into bright tomorrows. With this faith, we will be able to achieve this new day, when all of God's children, black men and white men, Jews and Gentiles, Protestants and Catholics will be able to join hands and sing with the Negro in the spiritual of old, "Free at last! Free at last! Thank God almighty, we are free at last!"

Five months later, after the assassination of Kennedy, President Lyndon Johnson's "War on Poverty" inspired Mayor Cavanagh. He was appointed a member of President Johnson's Task Force on Urban and

Metropolitan Problems. Cavanagh wanted to make Detroit "Model City USA" for federally financed urban programs—a coordinated approach to channel programs and services into the areas of greatest need. If they could obtain that financing, the city leaders intended to rehabilitate buildings in the inner city, create parks and community centers, improve protection by police, and build new schools.

Later as his police commissioner, Spreen had to refuse his requests that went against proper police professionalism four times, but Spreen still felt that Cavanagh was a man of decency and compassion.

Actually, very little government money awarded to Detroit arrived because it was drained off to the Vietnam War. White flight accompanied by high unemployment raged on. Edwards had moved on from his post as police commissioner, and his successor, Ray Girardin, had found the white police force and their attitudes toward blacks a hard group to control. Less than five per cent of police officers were black despite an intense recruiting procedure to add more.

Cavanagh ran for re-election as mayor in 1965 and received almost 70% of the vote. The following year he became the first mayor to head both the United States Conference of Mayors and the National League of Cities at the same time. He was riding high, considered as a presidential possibility, and was pictured on the cover of national magazines. One aide said, "On a clear day, he could see the White House."

In 1965, *Fortune Magazine* lauded Detroit for the progress it had made in race relations. In 1966, the head of the National Urban League added their accolades for Detroit's race relations and said that the city was on its way to being a "demonstration city" of race relations.

Early in 1967, Cavanagh noted that he was spending three quarters of his daily time dealing with the problems of the inner city. Nicholas Hood, Detroit's only black councilman, asserted in May, 1967, "With all of its problems, Detroit is far ahead of any major city in America because we have a city administration that will not only listen to the concerns brought to it but will set out to work on those concerns."

The Department of Justice called Detroit a "racial model" and the city received various awards and was called the "All-American City." Cavanagh was described as the "Dynamo in Detroit" who pulled the once dead industrial city out of its physical, economic and cultural doldrums. He was named one of the ten outstanding young men of the nation by the United States Junior Chamber of Commerce.

Perhaps Cavanagh was too heady! In the spring of 1967, police officers called in with complaints of "flu" in a strike intended to show the Cavanagh administration and the police commissioner who was boss. Only a month before the riot, Cavanagh said that Detroit had escaped much of the national civil unrest due to the city's responsiveness to the needs of the streets.

Cavanagh said Detroit's war on poverty was "the country's outstanding success story", lauded the program as "the best in America," and promised residents a "New Detroit." That was less than two weeks before the start of the Detroit riot. Rumors floated around that there were marital difficulties and that was corroborated when Helen Cavanagh, the mother of their eight children, filed for separate maintenance on July 18, 1967, five days before the riots began.

For Jerry Cavanagh, his dreams of distinction ended on the day of the riot. He did not run again for mayor. After the riots came the search for a new police commissioner.

On June 21, 1968, the day Spreen was brought into the mayor's office to discuss being the new police commissioner, he saw the picture on the wall of the mayor, his beautiful wife, and eight fine-looking children, six boys and two girls. He remarked to the mayor, "My mayor, you have a most beautiful family," not knowing anything about their marital problems. Later, Spreen was shocked to learn that the family had indeed broken up. The Catholic Church granted an annulment— amazing after eight kids! [When Mayor Cavanagh died of a heart attack in a hotel room in Lexington, Kentucky, on 11/27/1979 at age 51, his six boys were his pallbearers.]

Once Spreen accepted the job as police commissioner, which began July 22, he was glued to newspaper reports of Detroit events. There was one last thing that Spreen learned. Since 1963, there had been six Detroit police chief executives, averaging only a little over 18 months in office. No city can easily survive such police executive turnover without problems.

Police officers feel that they are the mainstays, and that they control their force while each new chief is simply tolerated for his short "visit." This is similar to a City Manager and his staff who are permanent employees and they simply tolerate the antics of elected mayors and city council members who come and go in many cities.

CHAPTER FOUR:
Police Commissioner of Detroit

On July 22, 1968, Johannes Spreen arrived to begin his job, taking the helm as Police Commissioner of the fifth largest city in America. It took great courage to accept this risky position in a "no-win" situation. Many had already turned down the position rather than have their names associated with failure and their careers blemished.

He faced a probable time limit of 17 months (the time left before the end of Mayor Cavanagh's term) to get things turned around. The choice of a police commissioner is at the discretion of each incoming mayor in cities such as Detroit.

After Spreen was sworn in as Police Commissioner, he found two things on his desk. One was a copy of John Hersey's book, *The Algiers Motel Incident,* which had come out the previous month. This Pulitzer Prize novelist captured the nation's attention with his slanted depiction of the beating and killing of three young blacks on July 26, 1967, during the four days of riots in Detroit. The book became a best-seller and added to negative views of Detroit police and "Motown justice". When Spreen arrived at his post, the officers charged with the killings were still on trial.

The other item Spreen found on his desk was a letter about the Poor People's Campaign, resulting from the Poor People's March on May 3, 1968, during which Detroit policemen assaulted demonstrators. The State Civil Rights Commission wanted to know what he was going to do about it. Tough beginning!

The next day, Spreen and Mayor Cavanagh walked 12th Street where the riot began a year earlier. Reporters were in tow. Being questioned,

Spreen remarked, "Where is the ghetto here? I see lawns. I see people raking and mowing. Hey, there are houses along 12th Street. New York in the Harlem and other areas had three, four and five-story tenement buildings. That's a ghetto!"

Mayor Cavanagh and Spreen dedicated a mobile recreation facility for the neighborhood kids, a huge truck trailer filled with water as a "swim-mobile," sponsored by one of the local television stations. The day was sunny and the kids were happy, splashing in the water. However, that night it was a different story.

Spreen's second night in Detroit was not many hours old when he was down on Twelfth Street again, this time in the darkness of the summer night, inside a squad car full of concerned top police command officers. They cruised slowly up the six-lane-wide street following a sweep of police cars, each with four heavily armed officers.

Spreen could feel the tension in the air in the eeriness of the too-empty streets and the rows of storefronts. He noted the expressions on the faces of the Police Superintendent and the precinct commander riding with him, and the rigidity of their bodies as they stared out the windows. Loudspeakers on the police cars asked the few people on the streets to disperse and they did so. Trouble that night was limited to some isolated fire bombings and reports of looting. A few scampering packs of youngsters were sighted, who disappeared before the police patrols.

At one point, the command car halted, and they had a standup staff conference on the pavement in the middle of 12th Street before returning to headquarters. Spreen got to know many of the ranking officers in the department in a hurry that night. The police alert for the riot anniversary lasted four days. There were a number of arrests, but no repetition of the disaster of 1967. The *Detroit Scope Magazine* in an article called "He Walked Down 12th Street to Stifle a Riot" covered Spreen's walk. Here's an excerpt.

> Caught in the delicate balance between sufficient force and restraint, Police Commissioner Johannes Spreen gave a commendable performance of agility last Thursday morning, during the 12th Street incident. Beginning about 12 p.m., with a group of youths breaking windows and setting two cars on fire, the activity slowly mushroomed until a tactical alert was

ordered at 2:30 a.m.

Commissioner Spreen, Superintendent John Nichols, Deputy Superintendent Charles Gentry and Sgt. Harold Liggett, aide to the commissioner, arrived on the scene at 2:45 a.m. By then there were seven fires—two suspected arsons and three started by Molotov cocktails.

Bullhorn in hand, Spreen walked the uneasy streets urging residents to return to their homes. He remained upon the scene until the tactical alert ended at 6:43 a.m.

In all, there were 16 arrests, mostly for breaking and entering and one for assault on a Tactical Mobile Unit officer. The officer, uninjured, managed to seize his assailant inflicting only a minor abrasion on his forehead.

Peace returned with the dawn and the weary commissioner departed 12th Street where the riot seeds were planted last July. Spreen has probably not seen the last of 12th Street, a place where scattered minor incidents mark a return to normalcy. Let's hope that when necessary, he can match the way he gently nipped last week's riot.

Spreen knew trouble lay ahead. Sergeant Edward Wolski, Jr., killed on August 5, 1968, had served for 18 years. Wolski was shot three times after responding to a "family trouble" call and locating a man who was firing a handgun. The sergeant was dead and two patrolmen injured by the time the suspect was subdued. The police were white and the suspect was black. News people were quickly reporting that Detroit was undergoing another racial confrontation.

The atmosphere in Detroit was very tense. Only ten days after Sgt. Wolski was killed, Spreen lost his second police officer on August 15, 1968. Officer Riktor Gutowsky, age 28, was killed when his patrol vehicle struck a bus while involved in a high-speed pursuit. The loss of a police officer is as serious to the man in charge as losing a soldier in war or losing a patient in surgery.

On August 17, 1968, black leader Richard Henry told the Detroit Republic of New Africa (RNA) members that signatures were needed to show that Detroit wanted to establish a new nation of Africans within the United States. Aware of this movement, on August 31, 1968, FBI Director J. Edgar Hoover wrote to Paul Stoddard of the Detroit

FBI office, asking his office to create a phony letter worded to screw up the RNA and cause dissension within the membership.

Mayor Cavanagh was under intense pressure to have a police commissioner who could perform miracles immediately. However, Spreen didn't know that the FBI was involved in unethical clandestine attempts to break up black factions within Detroit.

During the first week of September, bombings shattered the cars of two Detroit policemen. The explosions were caused by 10 or 12 fuse-lit sticks of dynamite, said investigators. Spreen ordered all-night guards on parking lots at all precinct station houses.

Throughout his short tenure in this disruptive atmosphere, Police Commissioner Johannes Spreen introduced a variety of innovations.

INNOVATION 1:
Police car bumper stickers

Before Spreen had arrived in Detroit, the *Detroit Free Press* had conducted a survey and found that Detroit's black residents were most worried about "police harassment and police brutality." Many suggested that police might not have been so brutal had they been more racially representative of the communities they served. Spreen knew that relations between black citizens and white police in Detroit required a major overhaul. He intended to recruit more blacks into the police force, but also wanted to change the perception of police to show them as protectors of citizens instead of punitive enforcers of laws. Therefore, he had "Protector of Liberty" bumper stickers placed on all police cars. He told reporters that it stood for POLICE—an acronym for Protector Of Liberty for the Individual, the Community, and Everyone Equally.

A Detroit police car with the slogan on the
trunk, "Protector of Liberty."

INNOVATION 2:
Scooter program

Spreen understood that a new role model for the police must be developed. He decided on a "wild idea" to get cops out of the car and back face to face with the public. He thought about his New York City scooter program. Why not here? He decided to try to have a scooter patrol contingent ready for the World Series in October, since crowds would be on hand to see the Detroit Tigers play the St. Louis Cardinals from October 2-10, 1968.

Spreen's idea was to re-introduce beat police officers in the form of a scooter patrol. He knew that scooter officers attracted the attention of children and citizens as they drove about slowly enough to stop and chat when appropriate. They could be known as individual persons by the community instead of faceless officers encased in the cocoon of a fast police car.

INNOVATION 3:
Approach citizens directly

There were problems from the beginning about how to fund Spreen's innovations, and especially about how to fund scooters. He never got a dollar from the city council members of Detroit, who refused all of his requests for additional funds for police.

He got his first 30 scooters from the Chamber of Commerce. He asked for them at a dinner at the Hilton with the C of C members, Mayor Jerome Cavanaugh, and Baron Hilton. His plea was heard and he celebrated the great day when he had 30 scooters lined up.

Commissioner Spreen demonstrates scooters to interested youths.

The image of the police was beginning to improve but the city council remained reluctant to support his plans.

In 1968 when the Tigers beat the Cardinals for the world championship, Spreen had been commissioner for only two months. Detroit, the underdog, pulled a big surprise, and had the city cheering for the first time since the 1967 riot. Everyone was out in the streets downtown. Detroit set a home attendance record and was called Tigertown, U.S.A. The Cardinals led the series until the final game, which was played in St. Louis. The "City on Fire" shut down to watch the game. The Tigers finally won their first series since 1945. Mayor Cavanagh, using the V for Victory, said the win saved the city.

When the Tigers won, black and white fans gathered at the airport to greet the winners. It was almost like a riot, but everyone was laughing. Spreen called it the "Happy Riot." The 30 motor scooters for crowd control were delivered just before the Series started. The streets were jammed, and travel was at a standstill. Police on foot were virtually limited to stationary observation. The patrol cars, symbol of modern police department mobility, were immobilized.

At the first signs of unlawful disturbances, the scooter patrolmen were the only police able to move around, and to respond. As a result, the scooter patrols made most of the arrests, and may have made the difference between a celebration that was contained before lawless elements could get out of hand, and something much worse.

The *Michigan Chronicle,* (Detroit's Negro newspaper) which is usually very critical of police operations, used a front-page photo of a Detroit scooter officer overcoming a gunman in the street, as an example of effective police service during the World Series aftermath.

In the following weeks, four other policemen were wounded in gun battles. Some ne'er-do-wells threw a lye-like material in the face of one policeman.

On October 29, 1968, Governor George Wallace came to speak in Detroit. Spreen and city leaders worried that the appearance of this racist would foment violence with dissident crowds. Security was very tight. A crowd of 9,000 showed up to hear Wallace—about 8,000 supporters and 1,000 hecklers. At the end of his speech, Wallace told the hecklers—mainly blacks, "You better have your day now because after November 5 (election), you're through in this country". That set the crowd going.

Another police versus blacks confrontation seemed imminent. A large crowd of several thousand milled around outside of the convention center, heckling the police and Wallace supporters and setting fire to a Wallace poster. After the crowd failed to heed an order to disperse, the police attempted to clear the area. A Tactical Mobile Unit officer was blinded by mace thrown by someone in the crowd. Even though 800 demonstrators battled 350 police, somehow no serious injuries occurred. Spreen had urged officers to use restraint. The police officers attempted to be impartial and tried to take only the action necessary to insure the protection of people at the site.

Among the anti-police contingent in Detroit was Sheila Murphy. She was a young white organizer for a group that raised money to assist Detroiters involved in police conflicts. In addition, Sheila received money from the Catholic Archdiocese to purchase video cameras to photograph "bad" police actions. She went to see Commissioner Spreen and was very anti-police. Spreen later wrote a column for the *Detroit News* that the Archdiocese should have also provided video cameras to the police to photograph the rebellious demonstrators who threw offal, wine, red paint, stones, etc., at police officers. Sheila married Ken Cockrel, the black lawyer who defended the killers in the New Bethel incident of March 1969, to be described later.

Spreen, like most big-city police chiefs, had a "honeymoon period" but his lasted much less than the usual 100 days. A real ugly incident occurred on the night of November 1, three days after the George Wallace appearance. The Detroit Police Officers Association (DPOA) wives organized a dance on the first floor ballroom of the Veterans Memorial Hall and over 100 couples attended. Also in the same building, the Ebenezer AME Church sponsored a high school dance on the sixth floor attended by a black audience.

This night Spreen had just come out of the hospital for surgery to remove a large (it was found to be benign) tumor from his right side. He had also invited the President of John Jay College to Detroit to speak to a club. After his speech, Spreen and his wife, Elinor, took their guest to the airport. Johannes wanted to walk him down to the plane but Elinor said, "No way, you're as white as a ghost. We must go home." Nevertheless, he protested saying, "Honey, we must go to the Detroit Police Officers Wives Association Dinner Dance." Elinor again said, "No! You've just been operated on. We're going home."

At the dance, some police wives alleged that some black youths from the dance had abused and/or insulted them. The interaction between police officers, their wives and the black youths occurred because there were insufficient toilets on the ballroom floor, requiring people to take elevators up to floors where there were more toilets. Word circulated that black hooligans were causing trouble on the elevators. Women complained of obscene gestures and sexual threats.

The result was that some teenagers were beaten and kicked, including some of Detroit's black elite. One 17-year-old son of a minister was hospitalized. He called his father who got to the scene while the beatings were still in progress. The 15-year-old son of Detroit's only black councilman at the time was an eyewitness to the whole affair. In addition to the beatings and kickings, a car belonging to a black had been hauled away. When it was returned, it was plastered with George Wallace stickers.

Meanwhile, Spreen was home in bed recovering from the tumor operation the day before. He did not learn of this travesty until the next morning. In the meantime, the press, radio and TV had a field day. The Mayor asserted that the "blue curtain of secrecy" was hampering an investigation of the police.

When Spreen awoke and learned of the incident, he was enraged at the actions of unprofessional police officers and was angry that police left the scene without taking proper police action.

On Sunday, he called the President of the DPOA to meet without the press. The President brought along his Vice President and Spreen really laid into them. He said those "police wrongdoers" had given much ammunition to the agitators against the Detroit police. He quite scathingly told them,

> "You tell me that some of the wives were groped, and grabbed by their breasts and rear ends, etc. Well, then, arrests should have been made and force used only as necessary. But you guys just beat them up and left the scene and smirked, and so left this fine city again on tenderhooks!"

The Common Council quickly grabbed the headlines denunciating police at the Hall commented that the FBI or State Police should be called in to investigate the Detroit Police Department. They demanded the appearance of Commissioner Spreen. He attended on November 7, 1968. Before answering their "eager" questions, he demanded the right to make a statement.

> If the facts as alleged are true then I can only express abhorrence and dismay at the actions of a handful of officers. I am further saddened by the knowledge that if this matter is not resolved quickly, fairly and equitably (with the principle of equal justice firmly in mind) that this can seriously reflect on 4,700 other police officers who were not there, were not on the scene, and I am certain are not in sympathy with such actions.
>
> The point that is missed by some police officers is that they occupy a unique position in society, because they are sworn to uphold the law, to provide protection of life and property, and to protect the human and civil rights we enjoy in a land of liberty, therefore, they certainly cannot be above the law.
>
> The Detroit Police Department cannot and will not tolerate any unlawful actions on the part of individual officers (whether on or off duty)!
>
> I ask that any member of this department or anyone that was at the affair to come forward and bring it to the attention of District Inspector James Bannon. I have issued an administrative directive to all members of the department to this effect.
>
> I feel that this department can and will conduct a full, fair, complete and impartial investigation and I want that opportunity.

Spreen was given consent to investigate his own department, and that he did. However, State Senator Coleman Young told reporters that some of the children had already requested that Wayne County's new 23-member grand jury investigate the incident without waiting. Young transformed the incident into another *cause celebre.*

Fortunately, Spreen was able to announce the results of his investigation within a few days. He suspended nine officers, fired three, and gained a little peace for the city. However, police morale dipped to a new low when the suspensions and firings were announced. Crime figures started to rise after a brief lull. An article on November 10, 1968, in the *Detroit Free Press* displayed the problems a police commissioner had in Detroit. Here are some excerpts.

Detroit faces a growing crisis over control of its police department and policemen...

Mayor Cavanagh concedes the crisis exists. So do Negro leaders, but they are not certain Cavanagh will exercise enough authority to cope with it.

The announcement late Saturday by Police Commissioner Johannes Spreen that department investigators have identified the off-duty police who beat Negro youths after a police dance at the Veterans Memorial last Saturday may alleviate some of their fears.

Nevertheless, the broad question remains: Who runs the department? The police themselves or the City of Detroit? The City Charter makes it clear who is supposed to run the Police Department: The civilian authority of the City of Detroit.

Recent events, however, have shown that Mayor Cavanagh and his new police commissioner, Johannes Spreen, are having difficulty asserting their authority.

Cavanagh complains that the police are not cooperating with the probe. Spreen had to issue a formal order to police officers requiring them to step forward with the information [about the incident].

The commissioner showed Saturday that he wants to command the department. The question now is whether the police rank and file will let him.

The issue was not entirely over, however, because the father of the 17-year-old who was hospitalized overnight filed a lawsuit against ten policemen, five officials and the president of the DPOA.

Meanwhile with the help of black clergy, the Detroit Revolutionary Union Movement (DRUM) secured a church to hold a mass rally on November 17th with a large community turnout. DRUM sold raffle tickets to raise funds and publicize the group. First prize was an M-1 rifle and second prize was a shotgun. Needless to say, law enforcement officials were watching DRUM closely, but from a distance.

INNOVATION 4:
Build rapport

Obviously something different needed to be tried. Commissioner Spreen embarked on one of the most unique managerial styles ever seen in a police department. Here is an excerpt of an editorial in the *Detroit Free Press* about it called "Rapport Is the Key".

Johannes Spreen is an exceedingly vulnerable guy. Anyone in his position who talks about things like "rapport" and "love" as the key to police work in Detroit puts his neck on the block.

The black man who complains that the cops are giving him a hard time doesn't want some high-powered formula for having X number of policemen at such-and-such a spot at certain times. What he wants is for the policeman to look at him without curling a lip and to give him a citation or make an arrest without insulting his manhood...

Or to turn it around, the policeman who wants "community support" really wants to be able to make an arrest without having his every move questioned.

In a word, rapport.

The test of Commissioner Spreen's stewardship will not be his goals—they are good, and he is painfully earnest about pursuing them—but whether he can make them the goals of men on the line.

Commissioner Spreen's scooter patrol has enormous potential for breaking down the hostility that exists. An arch-critic of the Police Department confessed to us a few days ago that the scooter patrol is working, and that even his own attitudes are being softened up.

But the officer out on the street still holds the key. He has encountered hostility so long that he expects it, and he is not likely to make the first gesture. Yet, if he can, in small ways, begin to break through the wall of prejudice, then he can build the rapport the commissioner is talking about.

Somewhere in between there is a better way. Commissioner Spreen calls it rapport, and that's as good a word as any.

Spreen's emphasis on rapport and love continued to grow and astound people over the next several months and will be recounted in Innovation 7 below.

INNOVATION 5:
Donate to help police

Realizing that he had so little help from the Detroit city council, but had support from citizens like the Chamber of Commerce, Spreen started a program called "Buck Up Your Police." In a direct and unprecedented manner, Spreen went to the people through media and reporters. He said, "If you care about your police, send one dollar to us." The Jaycees picked it up and ran with it, and the Detroit Police Department received $50,000 for scooters and other needed things.

Detroit Police Commissioner Spreen showing that $42,000 had been raised thus far with the "Buck Up Your Police" project he instituted.

INNOVATION 6:
Video cameras for training

One thing that the Buck Up project bought was video cameras. Spreen decided to instigate the first U.S. police use of video cameras for training officers by taping "Seven-Minute Seminars" to be shown at roll calls. The police had no training after police officers graduated from the police academy. Training in the ABCs (attitude, behavior and conduct) was needed if officers were to become more professional and less brutish. The cameras were spread across several precincts in Detroit as well as being placed in all police helicopters to assist in the capture and arrest of criminals.

Spreen also knew that police officers must combat attitudes of cynicism. After all, police mostly see the bums, pimps, prostitutes, criminals, and parasitic scum that abounds. However, they must also interact with decent, caring people that they protect. He wanted the press to give equal space to all sides of police interactions issues because media has a huge impact on a city's image. Therefore, he welcomed reporters and tried keep Detroit's positive image of police in balance with the negative image created before he came.

Another service funded by the Buck Up project was Public Information Centers across the city, each with a rack of brochures for the community. This was an attempt to help citizens by reading and talking with officers about how to prevent crime and protect themselves and their loved ones.

Still another funded program was a Citizens' Radio Patrol. Volunteers were trained to ride in twos through the community and report suspicious activity to police for further investigation. Their goal was "Observe, Report, Move." They were similar to the many sheriffs' posses of volunteers across the U.S. now. There were some 15 volunteer patrol groups ranging in size from 30 to 300 each, taking turns driving about and reporting trouble.

When Spreen took office, the police department's actual strength was about 10% under authorized strength, so the force had room for about 500 additional police. Of the 4,706 officers on the job, about 12% were black. The black contingent of Detroit then was more than 40% of the total population. To reach a comparable level in the police department would have required the addition of about 1,400 more black officers. However, among police applicants, about 13 to 16% of whites were successful, but only 3 to 4% of black applicants were successful.

Analysis showed that the written examination was the biggest single factor in the elimination of black applicants. If certain young people, from whom future police prospects were to be drawn, were receiving an inferior education, it was inevitable that they would do poorly on tests reflecting the results of schooling.

The police departments could not wait for changes in the educational system to turn out a larger number of better-educated young people. Different types of tests were sought that would eliminate such cultural bias, if that was the fundamental reason for the problem. An undercurrent of dissatisfaction was discerned in officers who felt that special examinations represented a lower standard than previous examinations. The touchy point was, "I want my fellow police officers to be just as good as I am, to back me up in an emergency. Will these tests bring in individuals I can trust in a pinch, individuals who are just as capable as I am?"

Spreen's difficulty recruiting competent black police officers was not the only problem with his staff. He also wanted police officers to be more professional. This professional officer would need sophistication and professional expertise, fundamental techniques of patrol, and a general understanding of sociological and psychological principles.

He encountered another problem whenever individual officers abused their authority: the "code of silence" kept them from reporting on each other. He argued that the "essential task is to create an incentive to break the code of silence among the rank and file and encourage cops to police themselves." He wanted to tell good cops they would be rewarded instead of punished if they exposed bad cops.

In December 1968, the trial of the officers and a security guard who were charged with killing three black men and beating others at the Algiers Hotel in 1967 finally concluded. An all-white jury found them not guilty. Commissioner Spreen fired the officers who had been suspended even though they were not found guilty. After the suspension and firing of the officers, the Detroit Police Officers Association came out against Spreen's decision and issued this statement, referring to the RNA goals to set up their own government. They issued this statement.

> The DPOA believes... the charges of police brutality are part of a nefarious plot by those who would like our form of government overthrown. The blueprint for anarchy calls for the destruction of the effectiveness of the police. Certainly, it must be obvious that every incident is magnified and exploited with only one purpose. A lot of well-meaning people, without realizing their real role, are doing the job for the anarchists.

Criticism of the Detroit police officers was stirred up again by the results of the trial. As morale of the troops sagged badly, Commissioner Spreen sent them a Christmas message excerpted here:

> This is Commissioner Spreen wishing all of you the happiest holiday season ever. In sending this Christmas message, I have an opportunity which doesn't come often enough—that is, an opportunity to say "Thank you" for your fine and dedicated performance every day of the year.
>
> I know from my own experience in the various ranks that policemen often feel that they have been forgotten—forsaken by the department executives and forsaken by the people they strive to serve. This will not be so in Detroit. It is my firm belief that good internal relations within the department are just as important as good external relations with the community, and I will dedicate myself to the improvement of both.
>
> I wish that I could thank each of you personally and tell you how very proud I am of you. Your excellent performance since I have been commissioner—a performance which is reflected in Detroit's remarkably low crime figures—shows that you understand and that I am 100% behind your professional

performance.

In this service, the hours and hardships of a police officer are perhaps felt more by our patient and understanding wives and families who sit at home and worry and wait…

Please allow me to extend my best and most sincere good wishes to you and your devoted families for a very merry Christmas.

Spreen lost his third police officer on Friday, January 10, 1969. Officer Stanley Rapaski was shot and killed when he tried to prevent a robbery at a bar while he was off duty. During the robbery, the bar owner told the two suspects to leave because Officer Rapaski was an off-duty policeman. The suspects instead went to Officer Rapaski, disarmed him, and then shot him as he lay on the floor. The suspects fled the scene.

As tragedies and criticisms simmered, William Serrin, *Detroit Free Press* reporter, wrote an article about the new commissioner's first six months, excerpted here.

When Detroit Police Commissioner Johannes F. Spreen took office in July, the 6-foot-5, 235-pounder was wished good luck. In his six months, Spreen has seen his 4,706–man department hit with three incidents in which police were accused of excess force against citizens. And at least 125 allegations of police misconduct, some of them substantiated, some not, lie on Spreen's desk from his Citizens Complaint Bureau.

Spreen clearly is on the hot seat. Liberals, Negro politicians—some sincere, some intent on grabbing headlines—say he doesn't go far enough to curb the racism that, in some degree, certainly exists in the Detroit department.

Police are angry with him for the 12 officers he has suspended so far. Even Spreen admits: "I've got a lot of policemen mad at me."

Spreen says unexpected incidents between police and Negroes have kept him from establishing the rapport he'd like to have with his men…

Says one top observer: "There's always been a saying among cops in Detroit. "We don't give a damn who's commissioner:

We'll make him do things our way or we'll break him."

Tom Johnson, an official of the Civil Rights Commission who is knowledgeable concerning police, says: "When it gets down to actually who runs the Detroit Police Department, I'm afraid you have to say the DPOA (union) runs it…the decisions the commissioner and superintendent make are influenced by what the DPOA will do."

As if that wasn't enough, the RNA was at work again. On January 18-19, 1969, the Republic of New Africa met in Detroit and the police undercover officer brought back several documents that were distributed at that meeting. They included a handbill urging the "brothers and sisters" to serve in the Freedom Corps, and pamphlets entitled, "To Build a Nation, the Freedom Corps Working Papers", and "The Freedom Corps".

In fact, *Esquire Magazine* published an article regarding the Republic of New Africa in January 1969, written by Robert Sherrill. It was entitled, "We Want Georgia, South Carolina, Louisiana, Mississippi and Alabama Right Now."

Milton Henry told the reporter that the RNA had 100 acres in Mississippi, that the method to take over Mississippi would be by electing sheriffs in counties with a black majority, and that "Having a majority isn't meaningful until the day comes when we have enough people standing at the polls with guns to protect our vote."

Henry continued,

In terms of real control of the land and real confrontation, there will be other things going on in this country. It could be burned to the ground while U.S. officials are playing games with us. They could be engaged in very costly guerrilla activities."

He went on to say that they could beat the U.S. Army with the aid of nuclear weapons from their allies such as China. He added,

We've got a second strike power right now in our guerrillas within the metropolitan areas—black men armed. Say we started taking over Mississippi—which we are capable of doing right now—and the U.S. started to interfere. Well, our guerrillas all over the country would strike. Our second strike force capability would be to prevent the United States Armed Forces from working us over, not the local forces.

If the whites defeat our objectives, the country will be ruined in the process… We can fight from within… The United States can be destroyed… This country will either talk to the separatists today or will talk to them later, at which time perhaps this country will have lost a great deal in terms of lives and property.

Henry showed reporter Sherrill two AR-15 rifles and stated, "We train regularly."

Obviously, the Republic of New Africa had been posing a more serious problem than the public knew. Unfortunately, the article also brought publicity and more recruits to the RNA.

INNOVATION 7:
Love-in

Spreen struggled to maintain fair play and community concern by recruiting more blacks. Just as he was about to announce a successful recruiting drive and a new budget to hire blacks, black politicos escalated a minor flap over a black teenager resisting arrest into a major charge of "police brutality."

Spreen tried to decide what to do in this tense atmosphere. He issued a document unique in police annals, an almost poetic dissertation on "love and crime." It called for a 100-day "Love-In" beginning on Valentine to unite the community and establish a moratorium on criticism of police until reforms could take effect.

Spreen was showing Detroit a role model of a man who could talk about love and care. He gave this declaration in his Valentine's Day speech in 1969 at the 12th precinct called "Love and Crime" showing where the community could help.

> The problem of crime is complex and difficult and requires competent, well-trained, acceptable, professional police and sheriff's departments to cope with it. But, if I had to pick one thing that could really do the job and solve the problem, it would be love.
>
> Love! What is it? It can be called a hundred different things, and the young don't have a monopoly on it. We seniors over 30 know about love also, and we are, hopefully, balanced by our experience. Maybe we can teach the younger generation a few things about love and work together for a pleasant and peaceful future.
>
> What is this love that can cut down crime and cancel community tensions? What is this love that can do more about crime than all your law enforcement agencies, vigilantes, guns and tanks? Let's try to define it:

- If it's caring about your neighbor so you report an assault you witness upon him or his home, that's love.
- If it's caring about your community so that you don't want to see if suffer, that's love.
- If you care about your fellow citizens no matter what their hue, that's love.
- If you care enough to willingly serve your country and your community, that's love.
- If you are concerned about the conditions that can tempt man to harm his neighbor, and you want to see them alleviated, that's love.
- If you get concerned about crime and do something constructive about it, that's love.
- If you feel that there are things wrong, injustices, evils in this world, and you earnestly wish to do something about them, that's love.
- If you want to change things that do not seem right to you, calmly, coolly, with considered judgment, rather than with a destructive "to hell with it all" attitude, that's love.
- If you do your thing well, within the law and within the bounds of propriety, that's love.
- If you put your personal desires and politics second to your concern for your community, that's love.
- If you concentrate more on helping to professionalize your police than to complain about or ignore your police, that's love.
- If you can take a negative and help turn it into a positive, that's love.
- If you follow the principles of honesty, truthfulness and fairness, that's love.
- If you use consideration, care, courtesy and compassion in your dealings with all you meet, that's love.
- If you live according to the Golden Rule, the Ten Commandments, or your moral, ethical or religious beliefs, that's love.
- If you consider the feelings of the other person as an individual who is with you on this small spinning speck of dust

called earth, that's love.

- If you have faith in people and in your police, that's love.
- If you have hope that we can all live together in a better world, that's love.
- If you offer charity to all your fellow men, that's love.
- If you believe there may be a spot in heaven for all, regardless of their race, color or creed, that's not only love but heaven on earth.

This startling departure from customary police rhetoric captured the attention of many. Bob Talbert of the *Detroit Free Press* wrote on February 21, 1969, "Spreen's Love-In: Here's Why We Can't Afford Not to Join."

Spreen's intention is to humanize the cop. He's taken some imaginative steps in this direction by demilitarizing the prowl car with his scooter-patrol Rangers, men with first names and faces that smile, who laugh with the man and woman on the street...

On July 22, Spreen took office, inheriting a department's troubled past, and an immediate riot anniversary confrontation the next day...

So Big John Spreen has now asked us for love.

He deserves this much at the very least. The man has some dramatic, innovative things to show us about what can happen when policing really works. But he didn't have them yesterday because he wasn't here yesterday. If we give him the time today to show us, he will give us a tomorrow that works.

During this "Love-In" period the best thing we can do is get to know our policemen. Invite them into your homes, your offices. Get to know them socially as people with first names and faces.

So what is this love that Johannes Spreen is talking about? He says:

"It's caring about your neighbor so you report an assault you witness upon him or his home. It's caring about your city so that you don't want to see it suffer. It's doing your thing well within the law and within the bounds of propriety. It's putting your personal desires and politics second to your concern for your city.

"It's helping to professionalize your police rather than policing your police. It's your never getting tired of asking what can we do to help. It's wanting to change things with calm, cool reason and considered judgments, not with destructive 'to hell with it' attitudes. It's having faith in people and police officers and the hope we can all live together in a better Detroit. It's making the policeman 'my man' not 'the man.'

"It's believing that a miracle can work in this city. The miracle of those silent, uncommitted citizens of our city speaking out and committing themselves. That's what love is. That's what it can be. That's what it must be."

Spreen has laid it on the line. You and I can't afford not to join his "Love-In."

The same day Talbert's article appeared was the anniversary of Malcolm X's assassination, one effect of the new calm resulting from this shocking new "Love-In" appeared to be the reactions to a provocative event honoring Malcolm X. On February 21, 1969, a rally was held at Northwestern High School in Detroit. The rally was to lower the flag of the U.S., to raise the separatist flag used by the RNA, and to rename the high school the Malcolm X High School. At approximately 4:00 pm, 250 people assembled, including members of the RNA. The green, red and black separatist flag was raised. School officials had lowered the U.S. flag earlier. Police were there to maintain order in this potentially defiant crowd but they were quiet, helpful subdued, and professional in manner. No incident developed despite this provocative action.

The scooter officer program begun in November was becoming more effective and very well received. These officers were proactive, not just reactive, and began to win friends for the Detroit Police Department. The "Buck Up Your Police" fund was creating a bond, a partnership with police, of old, young, black and white.

On March 7, Common Council member Nicholas Hood, a black minister whose son had been present at the dance incident back in

November, wrote this to Spreen:

Dear Commissioner:

> I want to congratulate you on the forthright disciplinary steps which you have taken in regard to the teenage dance incident at the Veterans Memorial Building, and the Christmas Day Curry case.
>
> It is such difficult and forthright action on the part of the police, which will also give them the kind of image, which is necessary for commanding the support of the community.
>
> Most sincerely yours.

A reporter wrote this humorous piece about Spreen for *Time,* March 28, 1969, entitled "From Detroit, with Love."

"Honeybun,

> Arrived in Detroit O.K. But on the way to talk to the people at Universal Inexplicable, I almost got smooched by a cop. Would you believe it!!!???
>
> Well, it seems this city got a new police commissioner last July and, boy, I guess it needed one. A year after those awful riots and all, the ghettos were still rumbling and the cops were being charged with brutality, inefficiency, corruption and so forth. So this new commissioner—his name, I learned, is Johannes F. Spreen, and he comes from New York City— announces a big-deal program of police reform. Tough new disciplinary standards, new equipment, etc. Mace? Hell, no! You won't believe it, honey, but Spreen's cure-all for crime is another four-letter word: LOVE.
>
> Well, as you know, I'm a founding member of the Peekskill Police Advisory Panel (PPAP), so of course I had to interview this Spreen. What a guy! Back of his desk was a huge Valentine from some high school kids inscribed: "Our cops are tops! With luv to the fuzz—Love—Peace—Have a successful love-in." So what's this love bit about? Well, Spreen explained, he had this idea for a 100-day love-in. For 100 days, he wanted all the wise guys to lay off the cops and give him a chance to make some changes. He said that if he had to pick one thing that

could really solve the crime problem it would be love. Great, but what does it mean? Well, says Spreen, "If you care about your fellow citizens no matter what their hue, that's love. If you do your thing well within the law and within the bounds of propriety, that's love. If you have faith in people and your police, that's love."

The next thing you know, honey, the whole city is behind Spreen. He delivers some pretty corny slogans, such as "Robins be welcome, robbers beware," but they eat it up here. Actually, the crime rate went up the first two months of the year. Seems it was a pretty mild winter in Detroit, and Spreen says the reason for the crime rise was that he didn't have his three best patrolmen working for him. He calls them "Snow, Rain and Cold." Ho, ho! Well, just as this whole thing is getting off the ground, Spreen starts another drive, this time for dollar contributions from citizens to help the department buy some new equipment. He's putting name tags on the cops, and he has them out walking a beat so the people will get to know them.

He's cutting red tape so that any police offenses can be reported quickly, and he isn't pussyfooting around with any cops who are found guilty of brutality. He just fired one, reduced a couple of others and disciplined a fourth.

Quite a guy, this Spreen. He's really changing things out here and making people love it.

Love, Your old man

P.S. Love to the kids, too.

INNOVATION 8:
Invited *four* agencies to investigate him

During Spreen's early months, there were calls for the Detroit Police Department to be investigated by outside evaluators. Rather than have it imposed on the Department, Spreen invited and hired outside advisors including the International Association of Chiefs of Police (IACP). The IACP studied the department and concluded that it was short of at least 1,000 men.

The City Council refused Spreen's request and justification for hiring more officers. The editor of the *Free Press* wrote an article about the confrontation and here are a few of the comments in the article:

> Louis Miriani produced the inane quote of the week when he said, "I thought we had a pretty good Police Department for many, many years. I don't know what he has done with the Police Department since he's been here."
>
> The answer is obvious if Miriani or the other council members would look. During his first months on the job, Spreen conducted the most effective recruiting program in the department's history. He introduced the scooter patrol, despite a great deal of ridicule, and the scooters have proved popular and effective. He's gotten more men on the streets, and is currently having an efficiency study made of the entire department, from his office on down.
>
> And he's been drumming up popular support for a dispirited department, meanwhile fending off the long knives wielded by Common Council and trying to make do with one of the most undermanned forces in the country on a per capita basis.

Commissioner Spreen also had problems with micromanagement

by City Councilmen as illustrated by a *Detroit Free Press* article in the same month entitled "Council Interferes with Spreen."

> In a week marked by more than its quota of silliness, one of the silliest statements was Councilman Philip Van Antwerp's hint that if Police Commissioner Spreen doesn't promote more detectives Common Council may charge him with "malfeasance or misfeasance" in office.
>
> What utter nonsense. It is precisely because of this sort of interference and restriction that the job of police commissioner in Detroit is so difficult. How does the council know that 70 percent of the detectives deserve promotion to sergeant?
>
> The police commissioner ought to have some latitude over promotions, and he ought not to be given a quota by the Common Council or by the detectives association. To impose this kind of restriction on him is to undermine his ability to do his job.
>
> If there is misfeasance in office, it may instead be in the council, which bartered away the commissioner's power to decide how many detectives deserve promotions.

Will Muller wrote an article at the same time for the *Detroit News* called "Jeers Switch to Cheers for the Scooter," excerpted here.

> Of late, there have been indications that the former New Yorker's dogged persistence in the face of recurring crises and city hall backstabbing is getting through, at least to the people, with his message: To win the fight against crime we must have the support of the community.
>
> There is, of course, the recent *Detroit News* poll, which showed 55 percent of all Detroiters crediting Spreen's department with fair enforcement.
>
> Last week, six women, led by an officer of the National Association for the Advancement of Colored People, went to the department and offered their best help.
>
> From the tenor of comment around the town's ordinary people, the same question is rising generally among those con-

cerned with living and working and feeling secure in Detroit. In the absence of leadership elsewhere, many people are looking to Spreen.

Every count was against Johannes Spreen when he took the job. He was an outsider police officer, a former operations director in the New York department, certain to be resented within the Detroit department.

He came at the call of a mayor in deep political trouble who had been hunting for months for a police commissioner to take over a city deep in racial trouble. Detroit, like every other major city, has a long reputation for pillorying its police commissioners in every real or fancied crisis.

Spreen has been here less than one year. It's something for Detroiters to say in a public opinion poll, in street discussions and by their actions that they have more empathy for him than for their own councilmen.

The Police Commissioner also had to deal with a "secret council". Reporter Mark Beltaire wrote about that "Our Secret Council" for the *Detroit Free Press,* excerpted here. Michigan did not enact their Open Meeting Act until 1976.

If Detroit's Common Council feels itself misunderstood, it can thank its own methods of operation for leading to that condition. All the hastily assembled press conferences in the world cannot make up for the fact that the council operates in secret. The real budget decisions were made by the council in informal sessions, away from the glare of public attention. Surely, in those sessions, there were shadings of opinion that the people ought to know about. Some individual differences were brushed aside in the drive for a show of unity.

There was more tension as Detroit hosted various Black Nationalist groups. Meetings and conferences were constantly being held, many of which fired people up against white control of the inner city of Detroit. It often fell to law enforcement officers to fight a losing battle to control crime and violence.

INNOVATION 9:
Help kids spend time with police

Spreen also showed up at many local events. He even made local events happen, such as creating a new program called Buck Up Our Youth (BUOY).

Commissioner Spreen painting with Detroit youth.

Commissioner Spreen wanted the children to be included in police activities as often as possible. He arranged an event for officers to invite children to sit on or ride the new motor scooters. His was a very personal style of interacting with the public. Police chiefs and commissioners often leave such activities to their Assistant Chiefs, but not Spreen. He had been inspired by mentors as a youth and wanted to do his part in helping mentor and serve as an example for as many people as possible.

Commissioner Spreen tried to involve public leaders and maintain their interest in helping solve crime problems in Michigan's largest city. One day he even invited the Governor to ride a motor scooter.

Unfortunately, the success of Spreen's positive programs and Love-In were short-lived.

Armed New Bethel Church attendees at the New Bethel Church before the shootout on March 29, 1969. Robert Williams poster is seen left.

The Republic of New Africa (RNA) held a meeting on March 28-29 that led to the worst incident during Spreen's term of office.

On Friday, March 28, 1969, about 225 persons from various parts of the country registered for the RNA convention. On Saturday, March 29, 1969, they met at Rev. C. L. Franklin's New Bethel Church to finish off the conference and celebrate the first anniversary of the RNA. Spreen's undercover agent was present. The meeting started at 8:30 pm and concluded at approximately 11:30 pm. As RNA officials left, two armed members of the Black Legion (the military arm of the RNA) escorted them. There were approximately 15 uniformed and armed members of the Black Legion present at the convention. Milton Henry, Esq., who ran the meeting as first Vice President, left the church at approximately 11:40 pm.

At 11:42 pm, a patrol car manned by Officers Michael Czapski (22) and Richard Worobec (28) reported to headquarters that there were men with rifles outside the church at Linwood and Euclid. Tragically, the patrol officers were unaware that an undercover officer was attending the meeting.

The two officers left their car to investigate the armed men, who had their backs toward the officers, walking away. The men suddenly turned and opened fire on the officers. Czapski, slightly ahead of Worobec, was shot seven times and fell mortally wounded to the pavement. Officer Worobec, who was struck twice in the back and once in the leg, crawled back to the patrol car seriously wounded and still under fire. He was able to press the car accelerator, and the car careened into a pole a short distance away.

The actual transcript (which is always recorded) between Officer Worobec as he was wounded and the Police Dispatcher was this:

March 29, 1969

11:42 p.m.	Patrol car 10-5: *"We got guys with rifles out here at Linwood and Euclid."*
11:42.50 p.m.	Dispatcher: *"Cars in #10 Linwood and Euclid. Men with rifles."*
11:43 p.m.	Patrol car 10-5: *"Help! Help! Ow! Oh!"*
11:43 p.m.	Dispatcher: *"10-5 needs help. All units—officer in trouble."*

11:43.20 p.m.   Patrol car 10-5: *"Help, help, help, help!"*

11:44 p.m.   Dispatcher: *"Two officers shot Linwood and Euclid."*

Officers arrived on the scene within five minutes and transported Patrolmen Czapski and Worobec to the hospital, but it was too late for young Czapski.

Minutes later, about 50 Detroit police officers attempted to enter New Bethel church. The black commanding officer, Vincent Evans, claimed the police were fired upon as they tried to enter. Once they broke down the door, police reported that they came under rifle fire from the altar and sniper fire from the choir loft, although the black arrestees later disputed these claims. The police arrested 142 inside the church, found 9 rifles, 3 pistols and ammunition.

Police arrested people from California, Illinois, Kentucky, Massachusetts, New Jersey; Louisiana, New York(including one man indicted in a 1967 plot to kill conservative black leaders Roy Wilkins of the NAACP and Whitney Young of the National Urban League), Ohio (including a man who had instructions for making explosives, sketches of uniforms, and a list of suggested military targets); Pennsylvania and Washington, D.C.

The rest were from the Detroit area including one who was a member of the New Detroit Committee in 1967.

In the cellblock after arrest, RNA organizer Richard Henry had the arrestees stand while he stated "Black power for black people. We accomplished more than during the 1967 riot. One pig down and the other one will never be any good." He was referring, of course, to the death of Czapski and the wounding of Worobec.

Judge Crockett, the black activist described earlier, told the press he was not sure that the Detroit police would treat these prisoners well so he established a temporary courtroom. Crockett began releasing those who were arrested, on either small bonds or personal recognizance, saying that those inside the church had nothing to do with the shootings of the two police officers outside the church. Judge Crockett had released all but two of those arrested. This included some who had tested positive for nitrate burns, found when someone fires a weapon. Judge Crockett criticized police procedures and invalidated their right to hold those arrested.

A storm of public controversy arose over the police "attacking" a black church filled with men, women and children [at 11:30 p.m.!]. Charges flew between the judge and the county prosecutor over the "premature" release of suspects. Police were caught in the middle and the city was divided worse than ever. The Detroit Police Department knew what had really happened, but was not at liberty to reveal it because it would have exposed their undercover man. The community simmered and a grim funeral was held for the dead officer.

When Judge Crockett released prisoners before police had a chance to process them, whites denounced him but blacks supported him. When a black activist arrived at the meeting of New Detroit and threatened to burn the city down, Max Fisher, chairman, convinced that the city was on the edge of a riot, announced support for Judge Crockett without speaking with Spreen.

Of those arrested, David Brown, aged 19, of Compton, California, was held for assault with intent to commit murder. Kirkwood Hall was held for possession of a gas-ejecting device. Subsequently warrants were issued against three RNA members. Black attorney Kenneth Cockrel, who belonged to the RNA, defended one RNA member against these charges. There were no convictions despite the death of one officer and the wounding of another.

Rev. C. L. Franklin never apologized for the New Bethel incident. He said the RNA would be welcome to meet at his church again, but he would prohibit guns. Days later, on April 3, 1969, there was a demonstration of 400 people at Kennedy Square supporting Judge Crockett's release of those arrested at New Bethel.

The bad press about the New Bethel Church shootout upset the Detroit Common Council and the police were made to look like they were in error when the suspects they arrested were immediately released. Spreen had trouble with New Detroit because they tended to listen to the loudest complainers. The squeaky wheel gets the grease!

INNOVATION 10:
House lights deter crime

On April 24, Spreen announced the beginning of a new "Light the Night" program sponsored by the Metropolitan Detroit Council of Real Estate Boards. They urged citizens to light up their homes during hours of darkness as a deterrent to crime. This idea has caught on and there is now a nation-wide "Light the Night" program but it was quite novel when Spreen introduced it.

At that time, most home invasion crime was committed at night. Authorities thought that criminals would be deterred from trying to enter a well-lit house. Statistics were showing some 4 to 20% less crime in well-lit neighborhoods. Not only did criminals stay away but also neighbors interacted outside their homes more with additional lighting, making it easier to see strangers approaching.

This practice changed crime and criminals. However, as time passed, criminals decided to approach houses in the daytime where owners were gone (to work) by ringing doorbells and entering if nobody answered.

Recently, it was found that parking areas at offices, malls, and stores benefit more by exterior lighting than do homes. Homes benefit by having lights come on when triggered by motion (motion detectors). However, Spreen was operating with the latest information at the time he inaugurated his new "Light the Night" program.

On April 26, 1969, RNA first vice president Milton Henry spoke at the National Black Economic Development Conference held at Wayne State University in Detroit. Spreen's undercover police unit covered these activities.

Henry described how he tried to be a "good nigger", his dishonorable discharge from the Army, his role in politics and election to City Council in Pontiac, Michigan, and the RNA. At the conclusion of his speech, he asked everyone to stand and raise his right hand. They did so not knowing what he intended. He asked everyone to repeat after him, then recited the RNA pledge of allegiance, and advised all present that they were officially Republic of New Africa members.

Among many speakers at the three day conference was Julian Bond, Georgia state legislator. He stated that the racist FHA refused to provide money for land procurements by requiring ridiculous credit standards for blacks.

Another speaker was Danial Aldridge, a substitute teacher in the Detroit School District and chairman of the Black United Front. His speech advocated the overthrow of the U. S. government, saying the only way blacks were going to achieve success was by taking such action, including the use of violence if necessary. He urged blacks to engage in groups to learn to manage and operate automobile industries to eventually take them over and then close them down. The plants have to be closed, he said, to destroy capitalism.

On April 30, 1969, Spreen made a presentation to a Common Council unaware of the dire plans made by the RNA conference that had just concluded. He described the Community Oriented Patrol officers (COPS) who were establishing more rapport with citizens. He told of the scooter officers who maintained peace at the World Series celebrations, the anti-war demonstration at Kennedy Square, patrols around schools and markets, Hudson's Thanksgiving Parade, and Christmas carnivals and shopping centers.

He was happy to describe statistics showing impressive drops in violent crime, auto thefts, robberies and purse snatchings in the precincts where the scooter cops worked. At that time, he had 76 COPs and 114 scooters in six of his thirteen precincts.

Spreen proposed to add more supervisory positions because aggressive recruiting led to some 800 new police officers with less than a year on the force. Spreen argued that they must have the supervision, leadership and guidance of well-trained supervisory officers but his request was denied.

The second week in May was designated as Police Week in accord with a national proclamation. DPD celebrated by having Open House at all precinct stations, and invited citizens to attend and visit with their police officers.

The Detroit Scooter Patrol interacting with children
on May 14, 1969, at St. Agnes School.

On May 16th, Spreen addressed the widows and orphans of Detroit area police officers killed in the line of duty. He was saddened by the loss of his fifth officer the following week on May 23, 1969.

After 15 years in law enforcement (13 with the Detroit Police Department), Officer Carter Lee Wells was killed with his own service weapon after making a traffic stop. Normally he rode a scooter but on that day, he was driving a patrol car. During the traffic stop, the suspect grabbed his service weapon and shot him. A passing cab driver who witnessed the murder rammed the suspect's car and held the man until other officers arrived. Unfortunately, the shooter was paroled after serving only 13 years.

Soon after the New Bethel shootout, Rev. C. L. Franklin was arrested for possession of marijuana as he returned from a visit to Mexico, but the charges were dropped. Then on June 10, 1979, Rev. Franklin surprised robbers in his expensive and historic home by some men who apparently intended to steal antique windows. He shot at them with his own gun but was himself wounded twice.

Of the six men arrested for the crime, one was granted immunity to testify against the others, one was given a 25-50 year sentence, and the others received probation. (Rev. Franklin went into a coma and died five years later on July 27, 1984. His children, including Aretha, spent great sums to keep him comfortable during that time.)

On June 18th, 1969, Spreen happily announced that they had 1,350 members of the Detroit Police Reserves. These civilians underwent training that allowed them to operate as the eyes and the ears of sworn officers and to summon officers to their communities when there was trouble.

In his effort to add good officers to the police force, on June 22nd Spreen began a program to contact servicemen with less than six months left to serve in the U.S. Armed Forces.

Spreen was asked speak with corporate heads at the National Industrial Conference Board's Conference on Crime and the Corporation at the Waldorf-Astoria Hotel in New York City on June 26, 1969. He described the tremendous help from the Chamber of Commerce purchase of motor scooters that the City Council and New Detroit would not approve. He described why close rapport between citizens and accessible helpful police officers was so important in Detroit where police were feared and hated.

Problems came to Detroit from all directions, disrupting the calm that Johannes Spreen was trying to maintain. FBI Director Hoover approved a plan for Detroit FBI agents to create a phony letter to pit black groups against each other and foment disruption in their ranks.

Another problem was that 25% of young black men were out of work, accompanied by an increase of 89% in Detroit's active drug addict population. Singers like Marvin Gaye made "Flying High" and other songs about drug addiction popular at this time.

Still another problem was those who demonstrated for welfare benefits. In September, Spreen's officers arrested 50 persons who were demonstrating with a sit-in at a social service center. They were members of the group of Welfare Mothers who thought they were receiving inadequate services. When they blocked the building entrance, the director asked the Detroit Police Department to intervene so they could continue to serve the public.

Yet another problem came from those against the war in Vietnam. The New Mobilization Committee to End the War in Vietnam formed two months earlier was said to be controlled by the Communist Party of the U.S.A. Detroit attorney James Lafferty, helped along with Common Council members to form the Detroit Coalition to End the War Now! Lafferty carried much weight as a spokesman against the U.S. war in Vietnam.

Despite these problems, the atmosphere of calm set in motion by Spreen was noted by *Time Magazine*. They ran an article about the Detroit mayoral election after the primary on September 19, 1969. It was called "A Victory for Reason" and stressed how blacks used their power at the ballot box instead of through violence.

The city and police prepared for anything and everything on the Vietnam War Moratorium Day on October 15, 1969. This was the year young people all over America were demonstrating against the Vietnam War. Spreen stayed on duty at headquarters and in the field on October 15, due to the planned marches and demonstrations conducted by the Detroit Coalition Against the Vietnam War, Breakthrough, and other groups.

Many demonstrators were en route to Kennedy Square in Detroit for a rally. On the way, they broke and shattered windows of a music store. John Nichols, Spreen's superintendent in Detroit, wanted to call out the riot troops using guns, shields, batons, facemasks, etc. Spreen countermanded his orders. Having had success with public acceptance of the scooter patrols, he ordered his scooter patrol to meet the advancing rebellious crowd and it worked like a charm. Not only did the young protesters respect and engage in conversations with the scooter officers, the scooter officers became an escort for them in their march to Kennedy Square.

The day was saved. It would have been different with riot troops. Many other cities had problems on the Vietnam War Moratorium Day but Detroit was spared. The demonstrations, mainly about 1,000 people wearing black anti-war armbands in a Detroit suburb at Chene Park, passed in relative peace and harmony.

Elinor and Commissioner Johannes Spreen, Deputy
Superintendent Charles Gentry and his wife, and Jean
and Superintendent John Nichols in 1969.

On October 18, 1969, the DPD opened a new Police-Youth Program in a building donated by the International Telephone and Telegraph Corporation. To raise money and attention for his new program, Spreen participated in a ballgame by throwing pitches to Detroit Tiger outfielder Willie Horton (and striking him out). He also threw wavering forward passes to former Lion defensive back Dick ("Night Train") Lane. The athletics were staged to kick off a physical fitness pentathlon that was part of the DPD's Police and Youth in Sports (PAYS) program. Spreen hoped it would bridge the communications gap between the youth of the city and the "establishment". He also used the event to distribute circulars about a curfew for children. He felt that 11 to 16-year olds out late without parents had to be safe and protected from potentially harmful influences.

Opening of new Police-Youth Program in 1969

In October of 1969, famed police critic James Q. Wilson quoted Mayor Cavanagh in an article called "The Urban Mood".

Detroit's Mayor Cavanagh indicates that "an administration is viewed not just through its mayor—but also through its police commissioner"…Perhaps the most significant phenomenon involving the police is the increasing political visibility of the police chief…Once a relatively anonymous public servant, the police chief has come to possess an "image" as important as that of the mayor, and the most successful chiefs are those practiced in the art of public relations.

Of course, Cavanagh was referring to Spreen and his role as police commissioner. The article did not mention, however, that Cavanagh had chosen not to run again.

On October 25, Spreen lost his sixth officer, Patrolman Paul Begin. He was shot to death and Patrolman William Skibo was wounded while they were transporting a prisoner to the Fifth Precinct. The suspect was handcuffed and placed in the backseat of the patrol car. Begin allowed a female acquaintance of the suspect to ride to the police station next to the prisoner in the backseat. She was not handcuffed because she was not under arrest. As they were being driven to the station, she produced a handgun and shot Officer Begin in the back of the head. Both suspects fled the scene but were apprehended several days later.

INNOVATION 11:
Using fingerprints

On November 6, 1969, the DPD was thrilled to announce that Detroit was the first police department in the nation able to check a suspect's fingerprints with the FBI. This was accomplished with a fax machine, which was very new technology then.

The FBI had developed cards with fingerprints of people arrested. They could then match the fax prints from a police department with those on their files. Spreen knew about their technology because he had attended special FBI training classes in Quantico.

It was not until 1972 that the FBI finally computerized their system called Automated Fingerprint Identification System (AFIS) that is now used across the country. These days, sending fingerprints to the FBI's AFIS program results in a hit in one out of ten cases, but in 1969, there were fewer fingerprints for arrestees. It was still worth a try in many unsolved crimes.

Spreen had many vociferous opponents as he tried to improve the police department in Detroit. Another veritable slugger was Mary Beck, the first woman elected to the Detroit City Council. What a formidable foe was she, a Ukrainian immigrant who instituted a "swear box" and taxed any council member who swore aloud. She became the first Ukrainian woman lawyer in America, first having been a social worker in Detroit. She served the Detroit Common Council for over 20 years, dying only recently. She led a recall campaign against Mayor Cavanagh in 1967 reacting to the four days of riots.

As police commissioner, Spreen found it very frustrating to deal with city council members in Detroit. David Cooper, a reporter for the *Detroit Free Press,* captured some of Spreen's frustration in a 1969 article entitled "When the Council Turns on the Heat."

Appearing before Detroit's Common Council is one thing. Making a presentation to the council without being interrupted by some councilman is another...

Last Friday, for example, Police Commissioner Johannes Spreen... took the witness stand... to make a major pitch for increases and improvements to the city's Police Department.

Spreen had a prepared text. He said at the outset he hoped to get through it and then would be glad to answer any questions. He had barely begun, however, before he was interrupted by Councilman Billy Rogell. Soon, other councilmen were jumping into the middle of Spreen's careful presentation.

At one point during a later discussion, Rogell told the commissioner, "Don't give me that stuff!"

Rogell's comment sounded more like something the former Tiger player might have shouted at an umpire whose call he did not like than what a councilman would say to a commissioner.

At one point, Spreen sat silently for 10 minutes, a slightly puzzled look on his face, as councilmen began a discussion of their own not directly related to Spreen's presentation.

Councilwoman Mary Beck was chairing the meeting, and kept relatively quiet until a TV cameraman placed a microphone by her side. After that, she was off and running.

Earlier last week, police department officials went before councilmen on a minor request. They wanted authority to spend $900 for a consultant who would aid in the computer program portion of a study of police procedures being made by Wayne State University.

The proposal was comparatively simple, but most councilmen did not seem to understand it. One of their problems may have been that various councilmen kept interrupting police officials during the explanations. Councilmen held up the proposal for several days, approving it last Friday, unanimously...

Of the city's nine present councilmen, only three, Mel Ravitz, Nicholas Hood and Louis Miriani, seem to try most of the time to listen courteously to city officials and to try to understand what they are saying. Two others, Tony Wierzbicki and President Ed Carey, listen sometimes, but occasionally join their other colleagues in badgering and harassing officials before they can complete an explanation.

At times, one of the city's new councilmen, Robert Tindal, speaks so often and interrupts so frequently that he seems to be trying to become the council's male Mary Beck…

When the Common Council learns to listen it may begin to fulfill its constitutional duty as a legislative body.

Mark Beltaire wrote an article called, "Our Secret Council" for the *Detroit Free Press.* He was quite critical of the decision-making method used by those planning the welfare of the City of Detroit. In instances like this, the press served the public well to reveal flaws in those they had elected.

If Detroit's Common Council feels itself misunderstood, it can thank its own methods of operation for leading to that condition.

All the hastily assembled press conferences in the world cannot make up for the fact that the council operates in secret. The real budget decisions were not made in those 22 votes of 9-to-0 to override the mayor's veto.

They were made by the council in informal sessions, away from the glare of public attention. Surely, in those sessions, there were shadings of opinion that the people ought to know about. Some individual differences were brushed aside in the drive for a show of unity.

What do the council members think the people of Detroit hired them for? Are some of them being made pawns by the candidates for mayor among them?

The last sentence referred to the upcoming election. It appeared that the Common Council wanted the public to vote out Jerome Cavanagh and vote in Roman Gribbs. As a former sheriff, Gribbs automatically symbolized "law and order". He ran on a law and order program to crack down on crime. He won a very narrow victory over black former city auditor, Richard Austin. It was the closest political contest in Detroit history. With only 7000 more votes than his rival, Gribbs didn't have a clear mandate from the people. Therefore, his victory did not ease the tensions; it exacerbated them.

After the November election, it was clear that Cavanagh would no longer be in office. Mayor-elect Roman Gribbs was reluctant to clarify whom he wanted for police commissioner. There were rumors that the mayor-elect thought a black police commissioner might bring more peace to Detroit.

As each day passed, Spreen had to decide whether to resign or to stay in the running for police commissioner under a new mayor. After a thirty-minute meeting with Mayor-elect Roman Gribbs, Spreen realized Gribbs was insincere and was just picking up ideas so he could carry on with some other police commissioner. When he came home after the meeting, Elinor asked Johannes what the Mayor-elect said. She also asked if they were going to be able to go on with a Florida vacation that had been planned earlier. That is when the frustrations piled up inside Spreen and the commitment to the community took second place to the commitment to his wife and daughter. Elinor, in her obligation to her husband, had packed up, left their home in Lynbrook, New York, and came to Detroit without hesitation despite many pleas by her friends not to do so. During Spreen's term, job demands in Detroit prevented vacations.

When the press caught up with Johannes after meeting with Gribbs, his exact words were:

> I have felt that some of the spokesmen for the New Detroit Committee, that prestigious group to which we all look with hope, have tended to undo with injudicious comments some of the good their funds were being spent to accomplish....
>
> The Mayor-Elect has not asked me to remain...so I can only presume he has someone else in mind. Also, I understand that in some quarters, I am no longer considered acceptable because of my color.
>
> Having considered all this, I feel that I have met my original commitment to Mayor Cavanagh and the people of Detroit, and I am consequently asking Mayor-Elect Gribbs to remove my name from consideration as the next Police Commissioner.

When the news aired that Spreen was withdrawing his name from consideration as the next Police Commissioner for the new Mayor, he received a copy of the following letter. It was addressed to Mayor Elect

Gribbs on December 5, 1969, from the 12ᵗʰ Precinct Community Relations Committee.

Dear Mayor-Elect Gribbs,

We realize that you must presently be very busy formulating plans before you assume your office in January. In spite of this fact, we write now because we also know that once in office, your schedule will be an even busier one.

As concerned and involved citizens of Detroit (and we do consider ourselves as such) we desire that you know and understand our feelings regarding Police Commissioner Johannes Spreen. We would like to see him retained in his position.

During the past two years, we have cooperated with the Police Department of the 12ᵗʰ Precinct through an organization we jointly formed, whose name this letterhead bears. This relationship was begun with the belief that this would help Detroit remain a good place to live, work and raise our families. Our close association with our police of the 12ᵗʰ Precinct and the other members of the Police Department in our city convinces us that we are on the right road.

On numerous occasions, we have collectively and individually received encouragement to continue, from Commissioner Spreen. He has, as a result of personal interest, encouraged and instructed the police to help us. It has, we feel, been a fruitful effort for both sides.

Our group is composed of members of all neighborhood organizations in the 12ᵗʰ Precinct, as well as interested citizens and businessmen. This area, as you may know, is comprised of approximately 120,000 people. We urge you to retain, with confidence in our support, Johannes Spreen as Police Commissioner.

Should you desire further elaboration on our position, we would be most willing to discuss this with you at your convenience.

Sincerely yours,
N. R. Litt, chairman
12ᵗʰ Precinct, Community Relations Committee

INNOVATION 12:
Reveal investigation results

Commissioner Spreen and the Detroit Police Department were unprecedented in having a major public institution so forthright about self-improvement and so confident in community understanding that it would lay the results out on the table. They had nothing to hide. Spreen considered these surveys to be management tools to improve police performance. Spreen gave a press conference on December 9, 1969, in Detroit, to describe the findings of the three investigations of the DPD.

The International Association of Chiefs of Police believed that the Department suffered from a shortage of supervisory personnel and uniformed sergeants for field supervision. They suggested that the department needed reorganization with fewer sergeants in the detective bureau. Common Council member Van Antwerp had argued that 70% of the detectives should be promoted to sergeant.

The two other reports commended Spreen's personnel and recruiting operations, but agreed that the police staff needed the help of trained labor relations experts to negotiate with police organizations and unions. They agreed that recruit training was good but more in-service training was needed after graduation from the police academy and Spreen certainly agreed. It was like expecting a doctor to pursue his career after graduating from medical school without any additional training or reading.

The reports expressed particular interest in the community-oriented scooter patrol innovation and suggested that it be given a full opportunity to prove itself. One report stated that the basic neighborhood patrol officer should be a well-rounded "generalist", which is exactly what Spreen was trying to do with his scooter cops.

The crux of the reports was that the department needed at least an additional 1,000 police, as well as additional radios, cars, cameras and tape recorders. The women's division was highly complimented by Arthur Little researchers for their preventive work with youth and their good rapport with the community. On the same day, that Spreen disclosed the findings, Lawrence Carino, General Manager of the WJBR-TV2 station, delivered an editorial on his TV station. Carino stated:

> Johannes Spreen's withdrawal from consideration as Police Commissioner in the new city administration was not entirely unexpected. Nevertheless, the reasons behind his decision should seriously concern all Detroiters.
>
> There has been, as he said, a disturbing tendency in some quarters to assume that police officers are guilty of some abuse of authority until they are proven innocent.
>
> There has been the negative attitude Spreen has so often encountered in his dealings with Common Council, with his constructive proposals for the Police Department too often lost in the endless bickering between Council and the Mayor's Office.
>
> There has been the frustration of having to spend too much time reacting to problems of the past, and too little in developing programs for the future.
>
> There has been the necessity of delaying needed improvements in the department until some outside agency completed yet another police study.
>
> More personally, Spreen has had to endure the pain of being told by his daughter that he is commonly referred to by her classmates as the "head pig".
>
> And now, presumably, Spreen will have the final disappointment of leaving the job just as many of the promising programs he put in motion are beginning to show results. And Detroit, in turn, will be losing a police administrator of uncommon vision and ability.
>
> When the burden of the Commissioner's office passes to someone else—as now appears definite—TV2 hopes it is a man who can serve the community as effectively as Johannes Spreen.

When the newspapers carried the news of Spreen's resignation, people wrote him letters asking him to stay. He was given a box of about one thousand letters after he made his decision. He found them poignant, touching, and heartfelt. If he had been able to read them all in early December 1969, he said he would have reconsidered his decision to remove his name as police commissioner. He was quite embarrassed about all this. He had no idea that so many people felt so positively and personally about him.

One particularly nice compliment had already come from Rev. Dr. Hubert Locke, assistant to Commissioner Girardin before Spreen. Hubert gave Johannes a copy of his book *The Detroit Riot of 1967,* and wrote the following inscription.

> To John Spreen: It's almost incredible the task you faced coming to Detroit as Police Commissioner exactly one year after the disaster which this little book describes. The fact that a year later you had achieved such major breakthroughs in building a bridge between the police and Detroit citizens, and healing many of the wounds within the Department, makes your tenure as Detroit's Police Commissioner one of the most significant in the city's history. We remember you with gratitude. Hubert   9 November 1970.

Spreen's numerous letters (over a thousand) may have set a record because it is a rare thing for so many individuals to write to a Police Commissioner. None of these people was asked, of course, to give permission for their names to be used so few could be identified. Spreen gave the author many of these letters and a few are excerpted here.

One thing that particularly touched Johannes was that every student of the fourth grade at Sumter School wrote him. A sample of one of their letters is from Bradley Scott D. "Mrs. Green's fourth grade class would like to tell you how much we appreciate your fine work. We are sad you are retiring. We wish you good luck in the future. We hope people stop calling you policemen bad names…"

> Mrs. John Theodorou wrote after her policeman husband died in a Detroit shooting: "I am the widow of the late John Theodorou who lost his life from one of the shootings Friday November 22nd, 1969…. I doubt if you remember but you met John and his little old brown dog in DeSantis's Parking lot when you paid your respect to another policeman who lost his

life, Paul Begin. John was very impressed by you and told me he hoped you were going to stay on in your present position. I now add my hopes to his that you will not want or have to desert our bullet shattered, blood spattered, body strewn aching and tired city." [Spreen remembered her husband well and wrote her about his memories of her late husband.]

Mrs. Hazel F. wrote: "Last week I saw two young patrolmen walking the beat on Whittier and Kelly. It gave me a wonderful feeling and I told them so…. These two officers seemed very pleased and wished that more people would tell them how they felt about them. The fact that they were there is another credit to you. How long will they be around when you are gone?"

Michael A. Y. wrote: "I think you have brought a warm heart to the leadership of the police department and thereby helped to humanize our idea of the police. There remains, it is true, a wide gap between our black citizens and our police, but I believe this gap has been reduced, at least among the moderate segments of the black community. Unquestionably, you have been the 'people's choice."

Harold F. Ewing, President of the Redford Shrine Club and James J. Spring, Grand Knight wrote: "It is with kindest personal regards and deepest appreciation that this plaque is being presented to you at our Inter-Fraternal dinner. We the members of George F. Monaghan, Knights of Columbus and the Redford Shrine Club and Masonic Order, salute and wish you God's blessing."

Linda and Gary G. wrote: "I was very sorry to hear of your resignation. My husband and I feel that you have done a fantastic job in bucking up the Detroit Police Department. You have taken a badly beaten department and transformed it into something we both are proud of….Now that you have made the Detroit Police Department something to be proud of, the job of Commissioner becomes a political plum."

Mr. and Mrs. George L. J. wrote: "My husband and I are two of many people in Detroit who are concerned for our children, our homes and our city. You gave us hope that the police can work in and with the community and perhaps there is hope and a reason for staying in Detroit. You made part of the news interesting and more exciting in that we knew something was being done to help us and our city."

A Redford High School student, Sherry W. wrote: "You are really 'with it' as shown by your groovy 'love-in,' in which Detroit gained some good favorable national publicity for a change. I am 15 and I think it is terrible that some of the other teens call the police 'pigs'. I feel that without police everyone would be pigs!"

John A. M., coordinator of the law enforcement program of the State of Connecticut, wrote: "I just read in the newspaper about Pat Murphy accepting your job. I'm sorry that you have lost out in the game of politics and hope that you have a suitable position to go to. If not, please contact me and I would see that you got hired on the September 1970 faculty vacancy on our law enforcement staff."

Attorney Walter S. N., whom Spreen had seen many times in court, wrote: "More than 75% of our contact has been on the basis where I was advocating the position of a client or clients. This letter has nothing to do with advocacy. In my judgment, your stay in Detroit was all too short. You accomplished much to increase the possibility of the Detroit Police Department becoming a fully professional institution within the foreseeable future. You have been the primary salesman in the community for the concept that just law enforcement is the only means by which the rights of all citizens, be they police officers or not, can be assured. Your constant seeking for recognition of the fact that with rights and power go equal and concomitant responsibilities has been inspiring."

Jay and Mary Lou L. wrote: "We need more people like you in leadership positions, who are not afraid to talk about love and bringing people together."

Harold G. D., who owned a bookkeeping and tax service, wrote: "I wish to express my personal thanks for your efforts to encourage law and order in Detroit. Also your constant reminders of the principles of 'love they neighbor as thyself.' ... Your police program has directed attention to our social reform program."

Mrs. James K. P. wrote: My family and I have enjoyed more trips downtown and into Detroit this past year than we had in the several previous years and I feel that it has a lot to do with our feeling that we had nothing to fear, thanks to the Detroit Police. If you haven't done anything else, it is so reassuring to see the policemen on duty either in patrol cars or on foot.... I liked your Buck Up the Police idea and contributed to it."

Pete K. wrote: "I am twenty years of age and a college student. I would like you to know that for the first time in almost two years I went downtown to see the auto show. You know what? It really felt safe down there for the first time."

Bonnie J. wrote: "I've never written a fan letter before, but I've been a fan of yours since you took office as Detroit's Police Commissioner.... You've brought a new vitality and enthusiasm to the Police Department. Your ideas have been refreshing and original. And you've helped give the police of this city a new, more humane image, which they really deserve."

Frank W. wrote: "Thank you for a job well done. You had style! You had flair! Your scooter program, the helicopter, the 'buck up your police', and the 100-day love-in were just great. I am truly glad you're staying in Detroit. History, later on, will bear testimony that you were right and the obstinate council, who had no guts, no vision, were wrong. The council couldn't turn the green light on. 'Hey, look about you' a saying my daughter told me about from Camp Dearborn last summer, reminded me of you. Soul is what it was. You made us all look up and around, and lifted our spirits high."

Physician Henry J. V., M.D., wrote: "I am certain you have laid a foundation for the development of a greatly improved department and respect for it by the people."

Mrs. Betty L. wrote: "One of the things I especially liked about you was the way you stood up for the men of your department. The police of Detroit have a very hard job and I think knowing you stood behind them boosted their morale and made them a better department. Another thing I like was the way you got out among the people letting them know you cared about them and about the community they lived in."

Judge John H. G. of the State of Michigan Court of Appeals wrote: "I am convinced that you have rendered a great service to the City of Detroit and have been one of the outstanding police commissioners Detroit has had over the past thirty years. The innovations that you have commenced with the Department are many. You have served during a most troublesome period and I think had there been a different commissioner, the racial tension would have been much greater."

A telegram from Dr. John F. B., the Wayne County Medical Examiner, read: "Your reasons for resignation are well-founded however I hope you will reconsider since the city needs you. You have done the best job yet."

President Rand H. of the Mayor's Committee "Keep Detroit Beautiful" wrote: "We had been so pleased with all you had accomplished for our city and were hoping you would continue with us."

Alison B. wrote: "I am a girl, fourteen to be exact, who is planning to be a policewoman. I read in the newspaper and saw on T.V. that you are leaving office. You will be a great loss to the police department. You're a very great man in my eyes. You have done so much to help combat crime in our streets. You have also proposed many good bills to make me wish I was of voting age to vote 'yes' on them....Here is a copy of a poem I wrote that my mom wanted me to send along. Being a Police-woman is what I want to be very, very much....Being a police-woman means helping not only those you love but helping all of mankind regardless of race, creed or religion."

Joseph J. W. wrote: "I am the son of a Detroit police ser-geant who retired several years ago, so perhaps I have more empathy for the kinds of situations you have had to deal with in your job. Both my wife and I are native Detroiters who love our hometown, but who also moved to the suburbs before you took over. Although we can no longer vote in Detroit, my wife travels into town each day and I come in two evenings a week to study at Wayne. Therefore we both feel very grateful to you because you have done the best job possible to keep the streets of our home town safe."

Elaine H., secretary to Queen's Blue Collar Workers of America, wrote: "As a result of your efforts to promote a better understanding between the police-citizens and the inner city, many are recognizing the importance of the attempts to estab-lish this line of communication."

Walter E. W., Service Director of the Marine Corps League, wrote: "May I commend you on a job well done and I am sure that had you stayed on as our Police Commissioner, this City would have become a safer one with less crime on our streets."

Thomas S. A. wrote: "I am a black man who has never written to a public official in all my 47 years. I feel impelled, however, to congratulate you for your efforts in regard to our police department and city as a whole. The best wishes of many thousands of blacks and whites go with you and your family regardless of destination."

Harrison E. B., Vice President and Treasurer of the Great Lakes Mutual Life Insurance Company, wrote: "I made several contributions to your 'Buck Up Your Cop' program with which to establish some of the equipment before denied you by the establishment. Detroit can hardly afford to lose men of your level regardless of capacity."

Mrs. Mamie M. wrote: "I only wish I could speak for the whole black race.... Whoever takes the job you are leaving whether his skin is black blue green white or grizzly would have to be a magician to deal with all the things I see going on in this world."

Annabelle L. wrote: "It is most refreshing to see my daughter return home from classes at Presentation Grade School and related almost a one to one contact with the motor scooter patrolman who had a class conversation with these children and give the image of the policeman that I knew in my childhood.... I am black but live in a world of human beings who benefit based on merit and not color. We also marvel as a community that policemen are no longer in cars but are walking and talking and meeting people."

A twenty-year city employee who did not sign her name wrote: "I am so sad. I am black. I feel you have done and are doing a grand job and that you have a real interest in the City of Detroit. You care!"

Ann M. K. wrote: "It is policemen on scooters, policemen walking and talking and smiling policemen everywhere... Actually life in Detroit has a new beginning."

Judith B. wrote: "It would be safe to assume that the book-makers in 1967 would have given the Lord Jesus better odds in bringing back Lazarus from the dead than you had in breathing life back into the Detroit Police Department. The men in blue are finally beginning to enjoy more public support and respect, all of which must be attributed to your community-oriented programs."

Charles R. N., elevator starter, wrote: "You may recall me as the elevator starter at the Hotel Ponchartrain.... I believe I am one of the few who have moved from the suburbs back to Detroit to gain independence and enjoy the many things and places that Detroit has to offer... Meeting the many guests and customers at my hotel, I extol the many virtues of our city in the way of museums, the fine Civic Center, theaters, parking and our fine zoo and shopping area and urge them to make use of them without fear...In a recent visit to Cleveland to visit old friends, I was dismayed to hear from them that they refused to visit downtown because of the black problem.... My sixteen year old son has never had any trouble and remarks about the frequency of police patrols on foot and in cars and scooters."

An officer who served under Spreen, Jim K., wrote: "I am proud to have served the Department under your leadership and I am especially proud that you were the Commissioner that handed me my new badge on 11-21-69."

Mrs. L. R. C. wrote: "On Nov. 30, we drove our family downtown to see the lovely displays and decorations. I can say with all honesty we felt safe, we have always gone down before, but we never could get out of the car. We were just plain scared. This year was different. We saw policemen walking and two others on their scooters."

Spreen knew by January 1, 1970, that he would not be police com-missioner but would remain in the area. Therefore, he decided to open the New Year of 1970 with good wishes to Detroiters. He thought he would return to teaching, and would do some writing and consulting. He would rediscover his family, and get to see more of Michigan beyond the boundaries of Detroit.

Helen Fogel covered the story for the *Detroit Free Press* on January 1, 1970. The story, "A Wish for Detroit from the Spreens" came out with a picture of Johannes and Elinor in front of their Christmas tree.

> The Johannes Spreens are wishing their adopted hometown a happy new year—and more than that...
>
> "I hope," he said, that this is the year we reach an understanding that we are all people—the black community, the white community, the police community. I sometimes felt I was caught among the three..."
>
> The Spreens came to Detroit 17 months ago where he took on one of the toughest—certainly, the most controversial job— in city government. During his tenure, he has worked intensely to maintain a high level of crime fighting, raise the level of police performance, especially in the area of "professionalism" and to stem the rift between police and the community and improve the relationship...
>
> He explained how, on Moratorium Day, the scooter men had been mobilized when some 50 to 100 young people out of the thousands who took part became "troublesome."
>
> "I shudder to think what might have happened if we had sent in armed, masked riot police," he said.
>
> "The scooter cops pleaded, charmed, cajoled the kids," he said. "The kids have got their arms around the cop," he said. "That's the way it should be with the policeman— always there, helping, aiding, guiding, advising," said the retiring Commissioner.
>
> "Happy New Year, Detroit."

CHAPTER FIVE:
Law Enforcement Professor and Consultant

A month after Spreen left his position as Detroit Police Commissioner; he was engaged to write a twice-weekly column for the *Detroit News* detailing his experiences during his tenure as Detroit Police Commissioner. He also returned to teaching criminal justice at John Jay College in New York and at Mercy College in Detroit. He flew into New York weekly to handle a full teaching load of 12 semester hours. Simultaneously, he was Director of the Law Enforcement and Protection Program at Mercy College of Detroit, which he continued until almost 1980.

His teaching theme was that we need police officers who both enforce laws and protect us. He called it "dual policing." Police must take proper action when crimes are committed, but must also serve as protectors and preventers of crime. He taught that if police are too separated from citizens (such as driving around in closed cars and not interacting with people) they cannot protect and prevent crime very well. He said we prefer human contact with known police officers *before* unknown officers speed to the crime scene *after* it has happened.

Spreen brought in some Detroiters to be guest lecturers in his police administration courses. He developed one course called "The Impact of Media on the Administration of Criminal Justice," with the author of the well-known book *Sybil,* Flora Rheta Schreiber. She was a colleague and English teacher at John Jay.

As college professor and director of criminal justice programs, he met Phillip John Stead, a visiting professor at John Jay College from

England. He invited Professor Stead to lecture his students at Mercy College. In 1973, P. J. Stead along with John Alderson, a well-known Chief Constable in England, wrote *The Police We Deserve.* That was something that Stead and Spreen often discussed at John Jay College. The community, in effect, gets the police they deserve. Likewise, the police, by their actions, get the type of community they deserve.

Spreen could recognize his own influence on Stead in the Stead/Alderson book. An example is on pp. 221-222 under the caption "Keeping the Peace or Enforcing the Law?"

> It is repeatedly proclaimed that the task of the police is to *keep* the Queen's *peace,* that state of tranquility in which our daily lives can carry on reasonably free from interference. It is *not the same thing as law enforcement.* Law enforcement is part of the concept of keeping the peace but by no means is exclusively so.

Spreen also recognized his very own words on page 12 of a later book, *Policing Freedom,* by Stead's co-author, John Alderson, in these lines which were Spreen's words: "The police have to be seen and to see themselves as *protectors of liberty* within the law. Freedoms depend on the ability of the police (and the courts) to *protect them equally, not unequally…*"

Spreen first used this exact expression in 1968 when he became Police Commissioner of Detroit. He had taught this to his students at John Jay College in 1970 and 1971 and explained his concepts to Professor John Stead and his Community Oriented Police Scooters (COPS).

Within a month after leaving as Police Commissioner, Spreen was selected by Oakland County Prosecutor Thomas G. Plunkett to "help bring big city experience and the experience of having tried new things" to Oakland County law enforcement agencies.

He was hired for a term of six months as a "consultant on law enforcement and protection" in the Oakland County prosecutor's office on February 11, 1970. He was a liaison between the prosecutor's office and police departments to improve communications within the law enforcement community. Plunkett announced that Spreen was available to all police agencies of the county for consultation on police services and training, subjects in which he was "a nationally recognized expert." He was to produce a document with proposals to improve any problems he found while serving as liaison.

While serving as consultant, Spreen wrote many articles about law enforcement for the *Detroit News* in his column. These excerpts give examples of his columns.

February 8, 1970: I was just starting my second week on the job in Detroit…We heard a report on our police radio that an officer had been shot at the Jeffries housing project. We were on the scene shortly before the first police cars responded. Three officers had been shot; one fatally, while they were investigating a complaint of 'family trouble.'

That night in August 1968, after the officers had been cared for, our first concern was to notify their families before the news could reach them through other channels… Police cars were sent to notify the three Detroit wives and to bring them to the hospital if they wished. Last October 25, for the sixth time, I joined a Detroit police family in grief, when I had to bring word of the death of young Patrolman Paul Begin to his wife and parents. I still don't know how to properly tell a wife that her husband will never come home again…

Police officers are neither angels nor devils, but human beings that have assumed one of the most necessary but unpleasant chores in community life; being on the spot whenever there's trouble. They never know when they will have to put their lives on the line. Respect them at least for that. It might help to console a policeman's widow just a little bit, to know that her sorrow was the community's sorrow.

February 15, 1970: Detroit's image is once again suffering and the morale of its citizens put under a new strain… Why is Detroit's image important? How many potential new residents decide not to move here? How many potential visitors never come here at all? How many groups hold their conventions elsewhere, despite the availability in Detroit of some of the nation's finest facilities?

The news media have special impact on a city's image and

a special responsibility. Too often, a city becomes stereotyped by reputation or events...Last October, a peace mobilization march was conducted in Detroit in a general atmosphere of calmness and coolness. I issued a well-deserved commendation to the entire department. But national television coverage gave a disturbing impression of the day in Detroit by focusing on one isolated 30-second jeering session between one speaker and a crowd that vigorously disagreed with his viewpoint...Media selection can hurt or help a city.

February 22, 1970: Today the pressures center less around which crime problems to attack first than they do around the ugly fact of tension between police and citizens, particularly black citizens... When the available resources are inadequate, which happens to be the case in Detroit and many other cities, the hard alternatives are either to secure resources equal to the tasks, find new methods to stretch what's available, or modify the tasks to fit the existing resources....

When events crowd too hard and fast, police and police executives have little opportunity to do more than respond. But prevention, not response, is the fundamental answer to the problems of crime and community tensions today.

March 5, 1970: ...It was no 'myth' that qualified black prospects were discouraged from seeking a police career because of the vehement antagonism of some of their peers... Some blacks now have called for an organized community effort to half the growing trend of 'blacks killing blacks.'...Crime hurts everybody, and it take a community effort to deal with poverty, social injustice, drug addiction, permissive gun-control policies, apathy and all other elements that make the crime problem what it is today...

The principle answer rests in the quality of the individual police officer and the opportunity afforded him to do a proper job. Then it will be up to that vast majority of citizens, black and white, to keep showing their support of a truly professional police effort.

March 8, 1970: Police administrators and citizens recognized that in too many cases throughout the nation, police themselves have been part of today's problem of community tension and crime, instead of part of the solution. What police are trying to do about it is to build complete and total 'professionalism' into the practice of police work...

The true professional cop is color blind, except when it comes to traffic lights. He knows when to use a handshake instead of a handcuff. He recognizes the difference between a nuisance complaint and a genuine call for help. He knows how to laugh when he is called a "pig." He knows when to hold his fire, when that shadowy shape he's pursuing might be a boy instead of a bandit...He knows how to correct a dangerous traffic violation without making the violator resentful...

The making of a professional may start with the police but the process isn't complete until the total community has had a hand in the craftsmanship.

March 15, 1970: Few policemen ever had as great a reputation for rapport with citizens as the old Irish cops of New York, Boston and other cities...The Irish cop was of the same immigrant stock as most of the citizenry, and served as an ideal buffer between 'old' and 'new' Americans. He tended to be tolerant of some infractions of the law, those that victimized no one...

My wife was raised a Fallon and her father was one of New York's 'finest' so there'll be plenty of green showing at the Spreen household March 17...

What happened when citizens decided to stop policing themselves, and to pay some of their number to become specialists in the functions? A peek into history should provide us with some useful insights... Such as the relationship between the modern policeman and a "walker through puddles", a town constable...on patrol.

March 22, 1970: Department rules require police to carry

their guns at all times, on or off duty. Detroit and New York police regulations say quite sternly and clearly that a policeman, whether in uniform or out of uniform, whether on duty or on his day off, who shirks duty in time of danger is guilty of cowardice. He is subject to immediate dismissal. A policeman is never really 'off duty.' I am sorry that police uniforms and weapons can have a disturbing effect on conscientious citizens. I think police officers should make every effort to keep their weapons out of sight and to wear them as inconspicuously as possible, particularly in off-duty situations. No good policeman wears a gun because he likes to, or flaunts it for purposes of intimidation.

June 8, 1970: Policing can be called one of the oldest professions. When God put Adam and Eve out of the Garden of Eden, and put cherubim on watch to make sure they stayed out, our first social order was established. Historians can trace police institutions back to the Code of Hammurabi, the Babylonian rule, more than 2,000 years before Christ… Rome under Emperor August was served by thousands of men called 'vigils', literally the 'watchful ones.'

Under Alexander the Great came…the social determination that maintenance of local 'law and order' was the responsibility of the people themselves, not the ruler. The people served as their own police, acted as judge and jury, and saw to it that any penalties or punishments were exacted. In 1066, specialists emerged to handle some of the duties of the law enforcement system—the most prominent of these were 'justices of the peace.'…The fully organized publicly maintained city police force is less than 150 years old.

Report to Prosecuting Attorney of Oakland County
Paul Gainor for the *Detroit News* wrote about Johannes Spreen's proposals to Tom Plunkett on October 22, 1970, a culmination of his recommendations after six months of interaction with agencies. Gainor began by misquoting Spreen and saying "Consolidation of Oakland County police departments has been urged by former De-

troit Police Commissioner Johannes F. Spreen." That was not true and created problems for Spreen with police chiefs in the county. The rest of Gainor's article is excerpted here:

> Spreen, a consultant to the Oakland County prosecutor's office for six months this year, said the county's present law enforcement structure is not adequate to meet increasing demands.
>
> 'What we have today is not the answer,' Spreen said.
>
> 'Many young people are dissatisfied with things the way they are, and young policemen are dissatisfied and have a tremendous yearning for professionalism.'
>
> He said his suggestions are contained in a report he has given Prosecutor Thomas G. Plunkett.
>
> He called for a 'task force' of federal, state and local police to deal with rising crime rates and street confrontations.
>
> 'What we need is coordination, consolidation of efforts and a working toward eventual consolidation of some police departments because no department can do it alone,' Spreen said.
>
> Also, Spreen said, a law enforcement and justice implementation team should be formed by police, the courts, prosecutors, youth and adults to 'get out there with the community and turn it on' to law enforcement. He said: 'What I propose doesn't take much money. We've got a start with very capable people who are now available.'

Prosecuting Attorney Tom Plunkett was so impressed by the work and report that he urged Johannes Spreen to run for sheriff of Oakland County. Spreen had studied and researched the sheriff's job as part of his report and thought that might be a valuable role.

Meanwhile, the new Detroit Mayor Roman Gribbs brought in Patrick V. Murphy as police commissioner. Murphy stayed only eight months. Murphy was tapped for New York City police commissioner in October 1970, a post he held until 1973. That fine man went on to become Executive Director of Drug Policy Foundation and has an excellent reputation. (He was a New York police officer for 25 years, and had served under Spreen as a sergeant.)

Gribbs decided to promote from within after Murphy left so quickly. John Nichols was selected to follow Commissioner Murphy. Therefore, by the time Spreen finished Plunkett's report, his former police department superintendent was serving as police commissioner.

The Decision to Run for Sheriff

Two and a half years after resigning as Detroit's Police Commissioner, on June 5, 1972, Johannes Spreen announced that he had decided to run for sheriff. Unlike his former positions, a sheriff is not selected or promoted. The citizens he serves must vote him in. Therefore, he must declare whether he is a Democrat or Republican. Spreen disliked that and said, "My own preference would be a nonpartisan competition for such an office because law enforcement transcends party lines and partisanship. There can be no room for politics in the administration of police services."

Members of both parties invited Johannes to be a candidate for the office of sheriff of Oakland County on their party ticket. He took the position that he would listen to whatever reasons they advanced in favor of him running for office. They were offering what amounted to a brand new challenge, and as he said, "Challenges are what life is all about."

What swayed him to run, he said, was that crime would increase if the concept of policing did not change. The challenge and opportunity, he said, was to guide and direct that change and over the four-year term, this would give him a chance to do that job better than the uncertain term of a police chief, which depends upon the term of a city mayor. With at least four years, accountable to the public, he was no longer a pawn in the game of favoritism played by mayors, city council members, and often even by police chiefs.

Like a doctor stepping into the midst of an epidemic and hoping to stop a disease and reduce the number of victims, Spreen wanted to also heal the suffering of survivors and eliminate future outbreaks. Could he be a Dr. Walter Reed during the Yellow Fever Epidemic. Could he be a George Marshall after WWII and restore peace in war-torn areas where disruptive forces had become commonplace?

Spreen told one reporter, "It all boils down to whether a man should teach his thing or do his thing. Should he be an analyst or a catalyst? I have come to believe it's more important to do his thing."

He decided to make his announcement at a press conference at his home. He set up a little German-style picnic with bratwurst, beer, and other goodies. Who better to help greet visitors than the Spreens' teenaged daughter, Betty, riding about on her motor scooter?

Spreen addressed those assembled:

> There is a problem of fragmentation of police agencies through the United States. There are some 40,000 different police departments, ranging in size from one man to New York's 30,000. There are all kinds of differences in selection standards, training, equipment, pay, and proficiency. There is an urgent need for a new approach to coordination and cooperation among the multiplicity of small departments. The sheriff's role provides support for smaller departments.
>
> It seems to me that the best opportunity for helping coordination among the small local police agencies resides in the office of the county sheriff, who already provides police protection in his county, outside the jurisdictions of municipal agencies.
>
> We know that effective law enforcement cannot stop at municipal boundaries.
>
> America is looking at its police more carefully than ever before, and it is time to reaffirm in the office of sheriff the countywide assurance of uniform police protection and equal justice that it originally implied.
>
> Because I see in the office of sheriff a challenge that includes an untapped opportunity for exploration, innovation, and service, I have decided to run for the office in Oakland County, and to enter my name in the Democratic primary.
>
> As a career police professional, I have always kept my political party and voting preferences to myself. It is an unfamiliar role to be publicly adopting a party label.
>
> I have chosen to enter the Democratic rather than the Republican primary after careful consideration. What ultimately decided the issue was that I had served as a law enforcement consultant to Prosecutor Tom Plunkett for several months dur-

ing 1970, and developed a great respect for his ability and integrity.

I do respect our two-party system, and the concerned and active members of both parties. I regret the need for party labels in connection with a law enforcement office. Law enforcement responsibility transcends party lines and partisanship. There can be no room for "politics" in the administration of police services. We are all entitled to equal protection from our official protectors in the police profession.

It has been suggested that I look upon election to the office of sheriff as a "four year contract with the people." That is what I seek. For the police administrator, whether he is appointed to a municipal post, or elected to county office, owes his allegiance and his responsibility to the people. That's the way it should be, and that's the way I like it.

I do not propose to run a "political" campaign, because I am not and never will be a politician. I propose to run based on my professional qualifications and experience, my educational preparation and development, and my continuing concern for the betterment of policing.

In addition, as I always have, I propose to campaign for aroused citizen interest, support and participation in the affairs of their local police agency. For only through citizen-police teamwork can any police agency be fully effective.

Johannes, Elinor, and Betty Spreen with Mayor
Orville Hubbard (r) and friend (l) in 1972.

Spreen had no sooner announced that he was going to run for sheriff when he was invited to give an address on Unions to the National Sheriffs' Association Convention on June 20, 1972. That year the National Sheriffs' Association created the National Neighborhood Watch Program to unite law enforcement agencies, private organizations, and individual citizens, in a massive effort to reduce residential crime. His reputation as a career NYPD executive, a consultant on law enforcement for a Michigan County, his term as Detroit Police Commissioner, and his influence at John Jay and Mercy law enforcement institutions prompted the invitation.

He told the sheriffs how some police unions are simply resistant to departmental changes in procedures and policies. Sometimes they challenge administration through strikes and work slow-downs, which weaken the overall mission of peace and order in a community. Sometimes their political involvement unduly polarizes a community. Sometimes their higher wage demands are unreasonable and unions become the refuge and protection of lazy employees and those unwilling to upgrade themselves. They may insist upon senior union members rather than the most qualified personnel for job assignments. They may even offer protection or legal assistance for those that are below professional standards within a police department.

He warned that unions could cripple police management so that the agency cannot effectively achieve its legitimate goals. In some departments, management has allowed employees to determine their own working conditions and the level of services to be delivered to the public. Other pressure groups in Michigan included trade unions such as the AFL-CIO. At state and federal government levels, such groups often hire lobbyists. At the local level, they use their presence, demonstrations, picketers, rallies, marches, flyers, and the media. They also use privileges and money and try to oblige law enforcement groups to favor them because they offer donations.

Another speaker to the sheriffs was Acting Director of the Federal Bureau Investigation, L. Patrick Gray. Gray, an ex-submarine commander during WWII, was appointed the Acting Director on May 4, after J. Edgar Hoover's death on May 2, 1972. Gray had a law degree and was Assistant Attorney General at the time, and was quite surprised with his appointment to the FBI. It was a great surprise because most people assumed that an FBI insider such as Asst. Director Mark Felt ("Deep Throat") would be chosen. However, President Richard Nixon apparently wanted a loyal friend to assume command. The overlooked Felt gave reporters Woodward and Bernstein information that led to Nixon's downfall. It later, of course, came out after Watergate that Nixon used Gray at the FBI to reward his friends and punish his enemies.

Unknown to Spreen at the Convention, only three days earlier on June 17, 1972, there was a break-in at the office of a psychiatrist whom Daniel Ellsberg saw in the Watergate complex in Washington, DC. When four men were arrested for the break-in, the police found much cash on them, papers suggesting that one worked for the CIA, and information showing that Howard Hunt was associated with the Committee to Re-elect the President (CREEP). They were attempting to discredit the military analyst and Nixon critic by learning about his mental state. The police were astonished when a lawyer appeared to defend the men, none of whom had called for a lawyer. The FBI was immediately involved in the investigation, which would ultimately lead to the resignation of President Richard Nixon the following year.

Gray later testified that John Dean, White House counsel, asked him to squelch the investigation. That comment opened the door to interrogate Dean and discover the great cover-up. However, all attendees at the convention were unaware of the role Gray would play as he gave his speech to the same group of sheriffs Spreen addressed.

Gray explained that the 59 FBI field offices across the country offered their services to state, county and local law enforcement agencies. Their Washington, DC headquarters offered a laboratory, identification and computerized information. Their facility at Quantico offered training of police officers, which Spreen had already sampled and found extremely valuable.

Spreen sympathized with Gray who had held this office for less than six weeks. Knowing law enforcement agencies, Johannes knew that as an outsider, he would have a tough road to hoe. Spreen knew that when law enforcement agencies got outsiders, that person didn't get much help from the agency officials who feel overlooked (as Mark Felt did).

Spreen listened carefully to Gray's seven-minute talk and was extremely impressed at his grasp of law enforcement, considering that he had never been part of it. He maintained that laws rather than men rule the country.

Gray stressed that the image of law is inseparable from the image of the men charged with its enforcement. A youngster's respect for the law centers on his admiration for that man. He charged the audience with ensuring that their employees maintain a record of solid performance, giving citizens full respect for civil liberties, strict conformity with due process, maintaining standards of integrity and service, and being impervious to scandal, corruption, and privilege. Local deputies and police officers are in a fishbowl where everyone can watch.

Spreen thought about Gray many times over the years. When Nixon's presidential tapes were heard, John Dean asked what they should do about acting FBI Director Gray, and John Ehrlichman answered, "I think we ought to let him hang there, let him twist slowly, slowly in the wind." Gray's testimony not only led to the demise of the Nixon administration but also to his own career in Washington, DC, but he later practiced law.

When Spreen returned to Michigan, he had to design a political advertisement to run in the local newspapers. That was hard for him because it required that he blow his own horn. Even though an ad says something like "Spreen Committee for Sheriff," the candidate had to design it because only he or she knows what they want to promise the voters. This was his first ad and it ran in the *Detroit News* on June 28, 1972.

Sheriff Who?

If you care who your next Sheriff will be, as we do, you will read this letter from our candidate…and help us elect him!

Dear Concerned Citizen:

On June 5, after many requests from sincere, concerned people of both parties, I announced my candidacy for the office of Sheriff of Oakland County and entered my name as a Democratic candidate in the Primary Election to be held August 8.

Why do I run?

Before becoming Police Commissioner of Detroit in July of 1968, we had never been in Michigan. We've found it a wonderful state with very fine people living here. We are proud to have made it our home. I have also found that the people of Oakland County are serious, concerned citizens who want better law enforcement and protection and if given the opportunity will help to improve our American system of policing and criminal justice.

I like police.

Police are in trouble in America. Rising crime and community tensions are twin problems that must be solved. Presently, no city really seems to be "making it." We need people to help policing and their police departments. I believe that the Sheriff, because of his unique position as a countywide representative of the people, can carve a new role in American policing to serve the people directly, and provide an umbrella of support for local police agencies serving them by providing supportive and technical resources and assistance so they can serve their local people better.

I can do the job—with your help.

As Police Commissioner of Detroit, I felt that I had the people's support for what I was trying to do. If elected, I would have a firm 4-year "contract with the people" uninterrupted by politics. Personally, I would prefer that this were a non-partisan election. However, I also believe that the people, through the office of sheriff, can vote on a law enforcement basis, rather than on all other political considerations.

If elected, I will use my training, my education, and my entire 33 years of police background to provide the best law enforcement and protection possible for the people of Oakland County.

How will I run?

On my record and background which I will present to the people. I am not going to run as a "politician" because I am not one. As I stated to a reporter June 5, "we will conduct an amateur campaign in the best professional manner possible, with the help of my family, my neighbors, and my friends."

You can help.

When asked how we could finance our campaign—"Would there be a 'Buck Up Your Sheriff' type thing" I laughed and yet, thinking it over, it isn't a bad idea at all.

"Buck Up Your Police" money (almost half of which came from Oakland County citizens) did many things that remain to this day. It provided operational help, training assistance (videotape equipment in all commands), educational upgrading (bookcases and professional books in all precinct station houses) and so much more.

Yes, "Buck Up" confirmed my faith in the people. I still

have that same faith and feel that if you think me best qualified, you will help me now.

If you believe as I do that the American sheriff can carve a new role and set new standards for protection of your homes and your communities, then please send what you can. Yes, any amount can help, and you can participate in the democratic process—you can Assist Better Law Enforcement!

Sincerely,

Johannes F. Spreen

The next thing Spreen had to do was to describe what was wrong with the Sheriff's Department and how he would fix it. He issued a press release that gave these points:

The sheriff needs to take a fresh look at all of his responsibilities. The sheriff needs to upgrade the police protection aspect of his role. This is why I am running for Sheriff of Oakland County.

I see the office of sheriff as an opportunity to help improve local police services. I see the sheriff as a catalyst to help local police units in Oakland County. He can help them in matters that require overall planning, cooperation, coordination of effort, and mutual assistance.

The sheriff is a key man in winning public support—an intermediary in securing greater teamwork between police, prosecution, courts and corrections.

Rising crime in the county is introducing more problems than many small police departments can handle alone. Without the sheriff's participation, their commendable efforts at voluntary cooperation are rendered haphazard and ineffectual.

With the mobility of modern criminals, one small community police department can't track them all down. However, countywide burglary patrol and investigation teams, spearheaded by the sheriff's department, could do something to change this picture.

Currently, the sheriff's department doesn't keep records of where the various crimes are committed. Without such basic record keeping, investigators can't concentrate their efforts. Furthermore, a basic manual of procedures and standard operating rules for every professional police officer is needed. This is the leadership's fault. Deputies tell me about that deficiency in the current sheriff's operations.

Another deficiency that bothers them is insufficient basic police training and no training for supervision and command. Another is the lack of encouragement from leadership to advance oneself professionally. Although there is a target range for shooting practice, there is little instruction in how and when to shoot. There is little training in first aid, a serious omission for those who make many traffic accident runs. There is no training in the use of department forms and accurate report writing, which affects court cases. There is no training in radio dispatch or the haphazard assignment of patrol areas.

Finally, there is no supervision of deputies on patrol to make sure they are doing what they should, no background check for deputy job applicants, and no exchange of information between incoming and outgoing shifts.

These were the things that Johannes Spreen set out to correct during his four-year term, which was successful enough that he was voted in twice again. He served a total of twelve years as sheriff of Oakland County.

CHAPTER SIX:
Sheriff of Oakland County, Michigan

Johannes Spreen was not an ordinary candidate when he ran for sheriff in 1972. For one thing, he pledged to keep Undersheriff Leo Hazen, the handpicked choice of the retired sheriff and the GOP candidate who ran against Spreen. Most candidates would have discarded a foe and chosen a new Undersheriff. In addition, Spreen, unlike his opponents, did not address groups by talking about politics. He preferred a more light-hearted approach using humor and discussing law enforcement.

He told the Southfield Rotary Club, "As police emphasis has shifted toward allegedly more efficient and impersonal enforcement of laws and ordinances," Spreen said, "psychologically and tactically police have moved from a preventive agency to a punitive one. In other words, police have been trending toward 'cold' professionalism when they should be moving toward 'cool' professionalism. It's kind of like the old Dragnet television series where Jack Webb constantly told citizens, 'Just the facts, ma'am'." He continued, "If police methods are genuinely efficient, they should not alienate anybody. Good police performance is the cornerstone of professional policing and it rests on a spirit of emphasis on service to the individual citizen, protecting him against becoming a victim of crime."

INNOVATION 1:
Changing the sheriff's program

During his first months as Sheriff, Spreen began to make changes in the sheriff's program.

1. He had his people prepare policies and procedure manuals because he found nothing on paper spelling out how a deputy functions.
2. He had basic law-enforcement seminars for deputies, some of whom have never had any formal training on policing.
3. He cracked down on the widespread abuse of special deputy cars.
4. He more than doubled the amount of detective manpower available without hiring any new men.
5. He introduced the Sheriff's Criminal Annoyance Team. Spreen announced that SCAT was designed to annoy burglars. Two-thirds of all crimes in largely suburban Oakland County were burglaries at that time.

"SCAT," said Spreen "is a wide-open crime-fighting approach specializing in high visibility. In addition to customary road patrols, uniformed SCAT teams in distinctively marked cars are being deployed and will do their best to attract attention."

He explained that instead of the usual report writing and detective work in burglaries, SCAT would concentrate on scaring burglars away or, better yet, catching them in the act. Spreen hoped that SCAT would help reverse a trend that had seen the burglary and larceny rate in Oakland County increase faster than Detroit's over the past five years. Spreen believed that burglars would be discouraged because "They know we're going to be there."

One early success of the program occurred when SCAT members infiltrated a luxury-car theft ring, which led to a massive raid and arrests.

Spreen had only been in office six months when he learned that Oakland County Prosecutor Brooks Patterson had been setting up a Strike Force to fight organized crime, which Patterson would run. He was doing this without letting Spreen know or working with him.

Spreen found that Patterson has gone to the county board with proposals that could affect his department without consulting with Spreen beforehand. One involved a request for sophisticated laboratory equipment for testing suspected drugs. Another involved an organized crime task force. However, Patterson did not have the authority to give his task force investigators police powers.

Spreen was getting a lesson in local politics as he gradually realized that Patterson was politically ambitious.

The Oakland Press covered the controversy in an article called "Does Oakland County need an organized crime task force?" The newspaper asked Brooks Patterson and Spreen to send in their views and printed the story on September 26, 1973.

A bitter disharmony developed between the two men. In fact, Spreen later learned that ambitious Patterson wanted to be *president of the United States.*

[Many years later, Brooks Patterson still makes news. Sheriff's deputies in June 2003 charged him with reckless driving. He admitted responsibility to a civil infraction (careless driving), and was sentenced to six months probation. The officers who failed to give him a Breathalyzer test (which might have been the basis of more serious charges) were suspended. On August 9, 2007, the *Detroit News* noted that Patterson encouraged Oakland County residents to buy automatic weapons or attack dogs "if they don't like guns" in response to planned changes in the State of Michigan's penal code.]

The Oakland Press published the article "Spreen-Patterson poll to aid Dems in county exec race" on July 18, 1974. It gave the statistics of a poll about the popularity of Prosecutor L. Brooks Patterson and Sheriff Johannes Spreen to guide county executive election strategy.

Poll results showed that almost 1/3 of voters said they didn't recognize Patterson's name but 83.8% said they recognized Spreen's name. Asked whether their impression was favorable, voters say yes for Spreen by 54.2% and for Patterson by 37.2%.

Johannes always encouraged women to enter law enforcement and thought they were particularly qualified to ride in his scooter patrol. In 1974, a lovely and enthusiastic 21-year-old young lady named Vicki Moreau became a process server for his department. She was awaiting the chance to work for the Detroit Police Department. He and his staff tried to interest her in staying with the county. However, she left when an opening occurred. Unfortunately, the young woman, who had just married David DeVries, was killed during an undercover narcotics raid gone wrong. She was a mere 29 years old and Spreen grieved when he read of her death as did so many who knew her.

INNOVATION 2:
Longer sentences for gun users

Sheriff Spreen's statement at the Senate Judiciary Committee on Senate Bill #127 on February 15, 1975, started the ball rolling for criminals to get a tougher (enhanced) sentence if they committed a crime with a weapon. It drew so much attention in Oklahoma and other states that Spreen was asked to submit his speech to the sheriff's journal. The June-July 1975 issue of *The National Sheriff* contained his article, "Can Crime Be Conquered?" Here is an excerpt:

> In 1938, J. Edgar Hoover spoke to the Detroit Economic Club. His subject was "Lawlessness as a National Menace." A few days ago, Clarence Kelley, the current director of the FBI, addressed the same body on that very same topic, asking the question, "Can Crime Be Conquered?" Sad, isn't it, that after 37 years the problem still exists, but to an even greater degree? Something *must* be done, and *now*, so that 37 years from now in the year 2012, we will not be asking, "Can crime be conquered?"
>
> I write these words not only as a county sheriff but as a police educator, with 37 years of police study and experience, having opened my first police textbooks the same year J. Edgar Hoover was in Detroit.
>
> I have seen the distressing toll in robberies, burglaries, rapes…citizens frightened and killed…policemen hurt and shot. I have had the heart-breaking experience over and over again of attending their funerals. In the past ten years alone a thousand law enforcement officers have been killed, and 70 percent by individuals using handguns. The fact is that policemen walk and work on the fingertips of death.
>
> There is no reason why this massacre—this uneven battle—

should continue.

The time for action is now!

Four years ago in May 1971, I wrote a newspaper column calling for an additional jail sentence for the carrying of a gun when it is used in the commission of certain crimes. I recommended five years mandated by law with *no* probation, *no* parole, *no* early release, and *no* good time.

We must do something about handgun control, but there is a vital difference between gun control and gun prohibition. We do not want to make criminals out of people who buy or have guns out of fear to protect their loved ones, themselves, or their homes. We are not going to accomplish anything by trying to ban all handguns.

We know that police cannot protect every person in his own home. We do not have the money or the manpower. We are losing the battle in the streets. Yet, we must do something—something better than we have done in the past.

Let us start by getting at the *real* problem. Let us get at the *criminal* who brings and uses a gun when he commits a crime. This is gun control. We need to punish the criminal, not the law-abiding citizen. There is a difference between a person who buys a gun to protect his loved ones and someone who is out to commit a crime with an instrument of death.

Certainly, the bum who uses a gun should not be allowed to thumb his nose at society. Let us remove these potential killers from the scene. Maybe, then, our good citizens will have a little freedom to pursue *their* happiness in these United States of America. And if these hoodlums are convicted a second time of using a gun in the commission of these crimes, the mandatory sentence should be doubled or tripled. The third time we should throw away the key!

The criminals, no doubt, always will be able to get a gun, and of course, the bullets for it, but if this legislation is passed, they will think twice before bringing a loaded gun with them when they go out to rob, burgle, and rape.

Who do we have committing crimes today? About three-fourths are recidivists—a small core who are committing the majority of crimes over and over again. And half of all serious crimes are committed by kids. Far more than half are drug addicts who are hopped up. Most of all, these people use guns. A gun should not be in such hands—hands which represent people who couldn't care less, or are immature or are crazed, hopped up by drugs, and whose fingertips could snuff out the life of a citizen or policeman…

Let us leave the gun-carrying burglar, robber, and rapist to his "peers" on the jury. Let him know that "if he does the crime, he'll do the time."

In later years, Spreen's support for enhanced sentences and its adoption by some states yielded significant improvements in crime rates. It was found that if a sentence enhancement is well publicized, it can have immediate effects in reducing crimes with a gun by 4% within a year. That was shown when California adopted Proposition 8 in 1982. A few years later, because these criminals were in jail longer (incapacitated from committing crimes with a gun) such crimes dropped by 8%. The effect continued to increase to a 20% drop in crimes committed with a gun by 5-7 years after passage of the law. This was shown by Daniel Kessler and Steven Levitt in "Using Sentence Enhancements to Distinguish between Deterrence and Incapacitation" published in *Journal of Law and Economics*, Vol. XLII (April 1999).

When Virginia enhanced sentences by prosecuting criminals who committed a crime with a gun under federal law, not only was an extra five years added to the regular sentence but also the federal prison required that the criminal be located far from his or her area (Project Exile). This well-publicized law was passed in 1997 and within one year, there was a 40% drop in gun homicides and a 21% drop in violent crimes. Ten years later, there has been a 46% drop in gun homicides, 65% drop in crimes committed with guns, and 35% drop in violent crime. The National Rifle Association has endorsed Project Exile.

Unfortunately, even though many states have such a law, they do not publicize it well or they choose not to enforce it due to crowded jails.

An incident undoubtedly involving guns attracted much attention from the Sheriff Spreen's Department in mid-1975. It was the disappearance of teamster leader James Hoffa. He was to meet two Mafia leaders at the Machus Red Fox Restaurant in Bloomfield Township, Oakland County, the afternoon of July 30, 1975. The case was taken over by the FBI and to this day, the details of Hoffa's disappearance are still unclear. A movie about Hoffa's murder with Robert DeNiro entitled *I Heard You Paint Houses* (referring to covering blood spatters on walls) is being released in 2008. Spreen always felt that the notoriety of such cases prevented good multi-agency investigations.

INNOVATION 3:
Contract policing

Spreen ran one of the first sheriff's departments who contracted deputies to work for cities with inadequate police personnel. Contract policing was so new in 1976 that Don Kubit of *The Oakland Press* ran a series of three articles exploring the advantages and disadvantages of contracting for law enforcement services with Spreen's department. (Meanwhile, John Nichols, the superintendent of the Detroit Police Department under Spreen had replaced Leo Hazen as undersheriff.) Here are excerpts from Kubit's third article on the subject, which ran February 25, 1976.

Oakland County Sheriff Johannes Spreen calls police contracting "the wave of the future. It is the best method of getting professionalism into police services," Spreen added. He said the "greatest virtue of contracting" was that it removed police from the influence of politics. "The officer knows the only reason he has a job is because people are buying his service. That job is on the line if he does not perform professionally," Spreen said.

Undersheriff John Nichols agreed with that assessment. "Police contracting is as close as you can get to a divorce of police and politics. The police are able to function in a political vacuum and are responsible to the people, not the politics of the township," Nichols said.

Spreen added that one of the strengths of the contract system is that the sheriff is the only elected law enforcement officer in the county. "If the people don't like what I'm doing, they can remove me from office," Spreen said. "But what can they do about an appointed police chief?"

Meanwhile, other heart-wrenching cases occurred in Spreen's jurisdiction. One of these was the kidnapping of 21-month-old Genevieve Rachel Nielsen. Her father took the little blonde 24-pound child with green eyes for an overnight visit on Mother's Day weekend of 1976. They disappeared. The father stopped using his Social Security number. In 2006, the father was found in an Arizona jail where he was serving a sentence for assault. That led to the discovery of 31-year-old Genevieve, who had been told that her mother was killed in an auto accident. Mother and daughter have been since reunited.

INNOVATION 4:
Open door for jails

Oakland County Sheriff Johannes F. Spreen promoted an "open door" policy at the jail by inviting groups to see their jail in action. He said, "I believe that the people are our real bosses, and so they should be able to see what they are getting for their tax dollar."

The first groups to accept the Sheriff's invitation were the Birmingham Optimist Club and the American Business Women's Association. "Members of the staff are donating their off-duty time to the program," said Spreen, "and we hope more and more groups will accept our invitation to tour the jail."

Spreen announced he would run for re-election as sheriff in April 1976. Since his first election, the political alignment of the board of commissioners has shifted from Republican control to an alignment in favor of the Democrats. That was helpful to Spreen who ran as a Democrat.

Spreen presented a handout of his county plans to the Oakland County Board of Commissioners on May 5, 1976. He made a presentation to them excerpted here. He referred to Governor William Milliken, who was the longest running governor of Michigan—14 years.

I had the pleasure of being invited by Governor Milliken to engage in a crime prevention conference yesterday. Polls taken by the Office of Criminal Justice Programs show two-thirds of the people in our state rank crime as the number one concern.

Crime and the fear of crime makes, as you all know, for a community image and a state of mind. A bad image is bad for business, bad for community growth, and bad for community pride. People despair and move to areas where they feel safer, and as a result, we all suffer.

What can we do? We must do something about the recidivist criminal, that small core who causes us the largest cost, who commits the majority of the crime over and over again. We must do something about the young people who commit half of all our serious crimes. It's shocking that the age of the most serious offenders is 16, exceeded only by 17 year olds. We must do something about the drug pushers who create addicts, who in turn commit so many crimes in order to sustain their habits. These three categories cause the most crime and the most problems and shame America today.

Thank God, we now have a mandatory sentencing law for the use of a gun in a felony in the State of Michigan, and other states are following our lead. It must become a nationwide concept. Let the word go out "You will be punished for using a gun to commit a crime."

It is only natural that the men and women in the Sheriff's Department have one primary concern—that of better, more efficient, professional law enforcement.

Let's continue to be tough on the criminal. Let's continue our efforts to prevent a crime before it occurs. Let's continue to educate the public in possible ways to protect themselves from the murderers, burglars and all criminals who prey on our society.

When the Detroit Police Department deactivated its Mounted Division, which traditionally led the Michigan State Fair, Sheriff Spreen volunteered the services of his 25-officer Sheriff's Posse. Undersheriff John Nichols and Spreen led the Posse during the parade toward the Michigan Fair Grounds. A picture and article about them was published in the October-November 1976 issue of *The National Sheriff* journal. Spreen whose nickname was "Scooter" was riding a horse he named Scooter, because the horse was born in 1963—the year Spreen introduced scooters in the New York Police Department.

Sheriff Spreen and Undersheriff Nichols led
mounted posse at 1976 Michigan State Fair.

INNOVATION 5:
Going to jail to defend actions

Sheriff Johannes Spreen was arrested and jailed for refusing to obey a court order. He was to reinstate a sheriff's deputy whom he had fired the year before. On March 11, 1976, he fired Detective Sergeant Keith Lester, 33, after the deputy was charged with failing to turn over $200 a court gave him to pay a crime victim. He pocketed $200, part of a $750 restitution payment made by three youths in a larceny case in which they stole a trailer. The restitution was to be collected by Lester and given to the victims.

Surprisingly, the charge against Lester was dismissed eleven months later. Lester then sued for reinstatement of his job and back pay of $20,000. Judge Thorburn dismissed the charge saying Lester should have been charged with embezzlement, not larceny. Oakland County Circuit Judge William Beer granted the request to dismiss the case. Spreen's view was that Lester was guilty. If he reinstated Lester, it would lower morale in the department. Besides that, Lester should have followed normal channels of appeal through the county employee appeal process to regain his job before he went to court. The courts had earlier forced Spreen to rehire four other deputies. He reasoned that if he continued to re-hire bad employees whom he'd fired, before long half the department would be less than satisfactory.

Judge Beer ordered Spreen to be jailed indefinitely on contempt charges. He said Spreen would stay in jail until he changed his mind and intended to lodge him in his own county in a local jail. Sheriff John O'Brien of Genesee County heard the news and sent his administrative assistant to suggest to Judge Beer that Spreen be taken to the Genesee County jail in Flint, Michigan.

The judge's order came late after a day of legal haggling. Spreen appeared at a press conference with a toothbrush in his pocket, saying that he was ready to be locked up for his principles. He told the reporters, "I never thought I would see such a day when I myself would be charged with a crime. But I'd rather be right than free." The Oakland County deputies later presented Spreen with a plaque that contained those lines.

Judge Beer, 67, who had been a judge for 20 years, said that Spreen had violated the separation of powers doctrine by refusing to obey his order. The judge told reporters, "Judges' orders, even if distasteful, must be obeyed."

Judge Beer denied Spreen's request to delay the jailing from Friday to Monday so that he could be with his wife, who was suffering with multiple sclerosis and curvature of the spine. She had undergone six operations during the last year and Johannes wanted to spend Mother's Day with her instead of in jail.

Judge Beer denied the request saying, "That has already been fully discussed."

Just before being sentenced by Judge Beer, there was a graduation ceremony in Spreen's jail for inmates who had attained their G.E.D. The Pontiac School system in their jail was teaching inmates how to obtain jobs and pursue a better life. Sheriff Spreen was scheduled to give the graduation address.

He felt that a motivational type speech was in order. The inmates did not know that he was going to be jailed that very afternoon. Spreen praised their efforts, told them they were started on a better road, and to keep going.

He then related the story of his life starting as a little immigrant lad from Germany who could not speak English. He told them about growing up in the Depression, gathering old newspapers to sell for a few cents, shoveling snow, and lugging boxes of wood to make a little money because his family was so poor. He described how he helped his father make cigars by stripping tobacco, how his parents hardly spoke English, and that he didn't go to college until he was 35 years old. He congratulated those getting their G.E.D.s and added, "If I can do it, you can do it."

He said, "When you get out, I don't want to see you back. Go out. Be a success. You can do it." At the conclusion of his remarks, he informed them that he would immediately become an inmate like them. He was very touched when they all stood and gave him applause that continued until Spreen left the room.

Before going to the jail, Johannes called his wife and told her that if she felt she needed him, he would acquiesce to Judge Beer's order.

She said very crisply, "Stick to your guns, Sheriff. We're all right."

Spreen swears that he will never forget that remark. She really would be all right. A contingent of officers from the Sheriff's Office was already at his home to offer assistance to his wife and daughter.

The sheriff turned his gun over to his undersheriff, John Nichols He was taken into custody by Kenneth McArdle, administrative assistant to the Genesee County Sheriff, John O'Brien. Johannes wasn't handcuffed, but Judge Beer had cautioned McArdle to treat him "just as any other prisoner in jail."

When Spreen arrived at the jail, Sheriff O'Brien welcomed him and they chatted for fifteen minutes before Johannes was taken to the booking area and fingerprinted.

A deputy checked his personal property, which included a wallet with $54, an uncashed paycheck, sheriff's badge, checkbook, tie, tie-pin, and shoes. His wife had packed clothes into a small suitcase, which he was not able to take along.

Spreen said, "I never violated a court order before. To me, this is kind of like a comedy, but it's a tragedy. All I know is my 35 years in law enforcement seem to be going up in smoke."

Sheriff John O'Brien, a fellow Democrat, arranged for an attorney for Spreen. His attorney, Robert White of Grand Rapids, began working on an emergency appeal of Beer's order. White told reporters that Spreen might be released the next day if he could get the appellate judges to hear the case.

They let Spreen keep his civilian clothes rather than wearing a prison uniform. He was placed in a cell apart from other prisoners, a 10-foot square room. The room had a bed, a desk, two barred windows, and was usually used for intake. He was in solitary confinement for his own protection. The idea was that some of the 303 prisoners serving time for murder or robbery might like to show a lawman what jail is like.

Johannes arrived after supper had been served so they got him a hamburger from a nearby Burger King.

Prisoners on the floor above Spreen called officers to control a disturbance during the 24 hours the sheriff served in jail. A group of inmates had overpowered a guard and stolen his keys. However, they returned to their cells after they found that the guard's keys did not fit doors that would let them out. Spreen was thinking, "Suppose they can't contain it. Suppose it gets down here? Would I be considered friend or foe?"

The sheriff slept from about 1 a.m. to 4 a.m. and then decided that was no good way to spend time. He got up and made some notes. Here is what he wrote at 4:00 a.m. on May 7th, 1977.

> You do a lot of thinking in jail. You think about how long you may be in, how long you will stay behind bars. You realize the importance of freedom. You think of your loved ones, particularly when they are dependent upon you and you cannot be there to help.
>
> In my case, you think of why you are here. How can you as a sworn servant of the law possibly be in jail for violating that law? You wonder at the strange turn of events, this strange paradox that has led me down this particular road ending up behind bars. Have I really flouted the law of my country? I guess I have but that was never my intention. And I would not say I flouted, I respectfully differed.
>
> How strange, I hear the sounds of people and traffic passing by and yet I cannot leave and join it. Why?
>
> My thoughts were on the protection and service of the people, under the law of our land. To do so with the best possible service under my constitutional obligation as the chief peace officer of the county.
>
> Yet this has led me into a collision course where principle met principle head on. Where I as an officer of the court had to object to its ministrations. I felt for the public good and the people I serve.
>
> Yet I am sure those same motives were in the mind of the judge who put me here. How odd; we are both attempting to do our job. Is there a greater morality over the legal letter of the law?
>
> I do not feel I really violated a law violently. I wanted to

pursue another road but that was apparently impossible. I do not feel unclean inside. I do not feel wrong. I did what I felt was right.

It is unusual that my 35 years in law enforcement and my earnest belief in proper and professional law enforcement have led me tonight to a barred cell in the Genessee County jail.

He also kept thinking about his decision. When Mayor LaGuardia gave Spreen the oath of office in 1941, he said there would be rough times ahead. He said the policemen would be looking down the barrel of a gun. However, he never said they would be looking through cell bars as a prisoner.

Supporters and well-wishers sent some 30 telegrams and made 74 calls on Spreen's behalf while he was in jail. One telegram from his own department read, "We are proud of you. Hang in there. The department stands taller because of your action."

Another telegram sent by the administrator of the Criminal Justice Institute in Detroit said, "All professional law enforcement personnel salute you as an administrator and as a man." That was very gratifying. Spreen put himself out there on a limb, and it could have been cut off.

Saturday he ate the normal prisoner fare of cereal for breakfast and hot dogs and beans for lunch. He talked with several of the inmates at meals. One, who was in for non-payment of child-support, told Spreen he would be perfectly willing to pay if his wife would use the money for the child and not for herself and her boyfriend. The sheriff thought it odd that we put a man in jail where he could not earn any money for child support. There has to be a better way, he thought.

Through the night, a 30-page appeal was delivered to a court clerk Saturday morning. By early afternoon, a three-judge panel of the state Court of Appeals freed Spreen on personal bond. They met Saturday and granted his motion to postpone the Circuit Court order pending appeal after the sheriff served 23 ½ hours. The judges set no date for the appeal hearing.

Spreen told a couple of the jail trustees who befriended him that they ought to continue their education. He said that if he could overcome hardship, so could they.

He was 57 at the time but he did what he felt was important and necessary. Spreen believed he had an obligation to law enforcement to try to upgrade the profession. He felt that Keith Lester had violated a trust and to restore him would be wrong. The public would have no trust in him.

When Johannes came home, his wife and daughter had draped yellow ribbons across the bushes and a large sign on the garage declaring "Way to go, Pa." He was able to spend Mothers' Day at home with them after all.

Sheriff Spreen was vindicated two months later by the Michigan Court of Appeals, which ruled that he should not have been jailed for refusing to rehire a fired deputy. Later, he learned that Deputy Lester was not only fighting his dismissal but was arrested on another criminal charge of willful neglect of duty.

Judge Beer, to his credit, later appeared at a party held in a restaurant for a fundraiser. He said to all that Johannes Spreen was a decent, honorable man; in effect that he, Beers, had been wrong.

Jim Fitzgerald wrote a very amusing article just after the jailing of Sheriff Spreen. On May 18, 1977, in the *Detroit Free Press*, he wrote "A Sheriff's Toothbrush Thwarts L. Brooks."

> The damnedest thing happened in Oakland County the other day. Prosecutor L. Brooks Patterson came to work wearing his sternest anti-parole frown, but he couldn't find one TV camera to put his righteousness on the 6 o'clock news.
>
> "Where are all the news people?" Patterson asked.
>
> "They are in Sheriff Spreen's office, looking at his toothbrush," he was told.
>
> Thus began a dismal few days for Patterson who, more than anyone, appreciates the power of publicity. He has become nationally famous by noting what makes people sick and then appearing on TV to proclaim that he is sicker about it than they are.
>
> If Brooks took the Pepsi test, he would vomit after sipping the Coke…
>
> Patterson speaks eloquently, with high emotion and magnificent indignation. He has made men cry, and he has made

them gnash their teeth. More important, he has prompted thousands of people to say: "That man should be governor."

In view of Patterson's popularity and ambition, it must have bugged him considerably when the entire nation, including Walter Cronkite, began talking about that gutsy man from Oakland County in Michigan—but they weren't talking about L. Brooks Patterson.

They were talking about Sheriff Johannes Spreen who got himself arrested and put in jail rather than compromise his principles.

How often does a sheriff get locked up? The media came running. Dozens of microphones were stuck into his mouth. Reporters begged him for quotes...

Spreen had fired a deputy for allegedly stealing some money. A judge ruled the deputy had been improperly charged and should be rehired. Spreen refused, thus breaking the law he is paid to enforce.

"I'd rather be right than free," the sheriff said after calling a press conference...

There was much applause and praise for Spreen's brave stand against the dumb judge. And, inevitably, it was said: "That man should be governor."

Johannes was proud to receive a letter from the Michigan Sheriff's Association on June 1, 1977, from their president, Bernard Grysen.

Dear Sheriff Spreen:

The Board of Directors of the Michigan Sheriffs' Association, on behalf of the membership, wishes to commend you for demonstrating the highest standards of integrity and courage for refusing to abandon the noble principles, which have governed your law enforcement career.

Your refusal to comply with Judge Beer's order to reinstate a person whom you believed had violated the public trust may ultimately be determined to constitute contempt of court. We offer no opinion as to the propriety of that act; however, we share with you a real concern that the high standards of professionalism of the law enforcement community would be seriously undermined if Sheriffs and other police administrators are required to reinvest persons who have abused the police power entrusted to them. We owe the public a higher standard of responsibility than to sit idly by and permit that to happen.

We sincerely hope that your position will be vindicated by the Appeals Court. You have our support.

After Sheriff Spreen was released from jail, he gave an address to the National Sheriff's Convention on June 20, 1977. He began his address rather humorously.

I don't know if I should speak to you today as Sheriff of Oakland County, Michigan, or as Prisoner #7702276, Genesee County Jail. This has much to do with labor unions and I will tell you about that.

Who really controls law enforcement today? It's those who have money. We in management ain't got much and the union has! We in management don't have dues paying members but unions do. Members and money mean clout!

Speaking of union power brings me to my own incarceration. Let me tell you about the "Lester case" in Oakland County and how I became a number in the system. I went to jail to uphold the standards of the law enforcement profession. I have now spent 36 years in law enforcement. I have had an unblemished record, and yet I wound up in jail with a number, was searched, my property was removed, and I was incarcerated like a common criminal. Why? Because I refused to return a man to duty as a sergeant, a man whom we had dismissed on charges of thievery. A sergeant should guide, supervise, instruct and set an example for those under his charge.

I felt I had to go to jail in order to uphold the standards, ethics and honor of law enforcement.

In addition to the emotional trauma of going to jail, there was some family trauma. My wife was ill and confined to a wheelchair yet the judge denied my request to make arrangements for her care before commencing to serve my jail sentence and sent me directly to jail. Yet, I would do the same thing again. If I had to choose one or the other, I would rather be right than free.

As the Sheriff of Oakland County, Michigan, in our department of 400 employees, only the sheriff, the undersheriff and the secretary are not union members!

We must believe in and retain our right to manage while recognizing our fundamental accountability to the public we serve. Let us be the managers of our enterprise and be the main man in that seat with our hands firmly on the throttle. We can certainly ride together with unions on the same track that leads to professional status of law enforcement, but we must control the train. That is what we were hired to do!

Much later, the public found out a very interesting thing about Judge Beer. He was discovered to have had nine kids in all, three by his first wife and six by his secretary. He led a double life for years until it was discovered after one of his children died. One of his kids (by the secretary) wrote a kind of gossip column in the *Detroit News*. A book about Beer called *Judicial Indiscretion* was made into an NBC movie of the week but with a different title and other names.

INNOVATION 6:
Intra-agency team for child killings

Spreen was invited to address the Southern Police Institute Alumni Association in Atlanta on July 29, 1977, about Oakland County's Child Killer investigation. Atlanta had been dealing with three Atlanta "Lover's Lane" killings. They asked Sheriff Spreen to address them because they knew about the Oakland Child Killer Task Force and wanted to learn what they could.

Spreen told the audience about some other murders near Oakland County. He described the two-year investigation of seven murdered Ann Arbor co-eds from 1967 to 1969.

They began with accounting student Mary Flezar on July 10, 1967, when she went for a walk one night. Police found her body on August 7. She had multiple stab wounds and her hands and feet were hacked off. Two days after her remains had been identified, a young man turned up at the mortuary, asking for permission to take snapshots of the body, which was refused. Employees at the mortuary could not give a description of the man.

One year later, on July 6, 1968, student Joan Schell was found dead in Ann Arbor, having been raped and stabbed 47 times. She had caught a ride with someone in front of the student union building. She was last seen July 1 with John Norman Collins, another university student. Her mini-skirt was wrapped around her neck. When questioned, Collins, a nice young fellow, claimed he was with his mother at the time. Police took him at his word.

In late March 1969, Jane Mixer was found covered by a coat in a cemetery. A law student, she had been shot and strangled with a nylon stocking. Two bullets had been fired into her head at point-blank range but there was no other brutality. Her jumper was pulled up and her pantyhose pulled off but she had not been sexually assaulted or stabbed.

That same month, construction workers near the scene of Schell's murder found another victim. A 16-year-old named Maralynn Skelton who had been hitchhiking was killed by crushing blows about the head. A garter belt had been twisted around her neck. A stick had been rammed into her vagina, and police reported evidence of flogging with a heavy strap or belt before she died.

About three weeks later, 13-year-old Dawn Basom was found half-naked in Superior Township, strangled with a black electric cord. The eighth grade student's body was slashed across the breasts and buttocks with a razor or very sharp knife. A handkerchief was stuffed into her mouth and her blue stretch pants were missing. She had been reported missing by her mother on April 18, when she failed to return home from visiting a friend. She was last seen walking down the Penn Central Railroad tracks, which passed near her house.

On June 9, 1969, some teen-aged boys found college Alice Kalom in a vacant field near Ypsilanti. She had been raped and stabbed repeatedly, her throat slashed, with a bullet in her brain. The public outcry was increasing but they had no leads. Spreen described how a psychic was brought in, but proved to be of little help.

Soon the police had another victim, 18-year-old freshman student Karen Sue Bieneman. She was declared missing on July 23, 1969, and was found a few days later, strangled and beaten to death, her breasts and stomach scalded with a caustic liquid. Her panties had been stuffed into her vagina with short, clipped hairs from someone other than the victim included.

While waiting for her on the day she disappeared, a shop manager saw her companion on his motorcycle. Bieneman had told her that she did a foolish thing—accepting a ride with a stranger on a motorcycle. She then exited the store and left with this unknown person on the motorcycle believed to be a Honda 450. Investigators obtained a list of all Honda 450s in the state and attempted to find the killer through this list. Investigations led to John Collins, who was arrested but denied guilt as he had before. During the investigation police found that he had a history of sexual harassment. The only murder Collins was prosecuted for was that of Karen Sue Bieneman. He was sentenced to life in prison in August of 1970.

[Interestingly, a movie called *Now I Lay Me Down to Sleep* about the murders was based on Edward Keyes book *The Michigan Murders.* Collins complained the movie project could jeopardize his fight for freedom during the appeal process. Movie producer William Martin promised that he would stop production if Collins asked for and passed a lie detector test, which he never did.]

Spreen finally got to the murders of children in Oakland County. He told of seven children murdered within a very short time. At least four were believed to be the work of the same person or persons.

Sheriff Spreen described Oakland County as one of the wealthiest counties in the U.S. It consists of small communities and rural farmland. Its population is composed of General Motors executives, business people, factory workers, farmers, and various professionals. The kidnapping of Jimmy Hoffa from a nice restaurant made news. But it was not as personal and revolting as the murder of these children and young women. The supposedly distant problem crime problem hit home. Spreen described the law enforcement in Oakland County as extremely fragmented. He said there were 43 police agencies in the county ranging from five man departments to the City of Pontiac with 200 police officers.

"Each police agency," said Spreen, "jealously guards their bailiwick from encroachment by other agencies as a king would his kingdom." This fragmentation became a horror story in the murder investigation as two sheriffs' departments, state police, the FBI, and eight local police departments were directly involved. In addition, two medical examiners' offices, three crime labs, and two prosecutors' offices worked on these crimes.

On February 15, 1976, 12 year-old Mark Stebbins was reported missing. Four officers handled it as a runaway until the next day when circumstances made them suspect foul play. Four days later, his body was found next to a dumpster. The state police and county crime labs were not called to process the scene. By the time the county medical examiner's office arrived, the body had been unclothed and taken to the police department rather than the county morgue. The killer had not tried to conceal the body. It did not immediately appear that Mark was sexually abused, but later post-mortem disclosed that he was. "No one knows what might have been found at the scene had proper crime scene procedures been followed and a crime lab involved," Spreen stressed.

On December 22, 1976, 12 year-old Jill Robinson left her home after arguing with her mother. It was believed that she rode her bike to her father's home a few miles away. When she did not arrive, she was reported missing by her mother. Four days later, her body was found 200 yards from a police station. She had died from a shotgun blast to the head. Again, no crime lab was called to process the scene. Again, there were no attempts to conceal the body and no apparent evidence that she was sexually abused. The head and face were blown off.

Noting the similarities of the two cases, Spreen and others suggested that a coordinated effort involving state police, sheriff and local authorities be implemented, but the offer was declined by the local agencies.

A week later, 10 year-old Kristine Mihelich went to a nearby store January 2, 1977. She was reported missing after a short time. Fearing the worst, two detectives initiated a search and the body was found some days later. She had been suffocated and gently placed next to a street. She was fully clothed and still wearing her backpack. Again, there was no positive evidence of sexual abuse. Her body was deposited in a very small community with only a five-man department where the crime scene could not be protected from traffic, onlookers, media, etc. The chief, having no personal experience in homicide investigation, turned the matter over to the State Police who then requested assistance from area departments. That afternoon, 30 investigators formed the Oakland Task Force and committed themselves to finding the girl's murderer.

The Sheriff's Department crime lab processed the girl's room for evidence. Hundreds of leads came in but by March 1, only 11 investigators were sifting through 800 tips and trying to solve the crime. It was discovered that one jurisdiction had virtually no report and in another jurisdiction, evidence had been misplaced and mishandled. Another agency was reluctant to submit their report to the Task Force.

Spreen detailed to the group how the Task Force was hampered from the start by each jurisdiction's different procedures. The press allowed a politically ambitious prosecutor to assume the role of coordinator and spokesman. A Canadian crime expert was summoned to handle fingerprints when Spreen's department could have handled that task. His fingerprint investigator was just as qualified and was used by the City of Detroit for all their questionable homicides.

On March 16, 1977, 11 year-old Timothy King left his home to go to a corner drugstore. He was reported missing that evening. The next morning, Task Force members were sent to coordinate the investigation. The news media put the public into a state of fear saying that a maniac child killer was on the loose.

The Task Force recognized that they might have no longer than four days to find Timothy alive. That evening, 300 investigators converged to find Timmy. They stopped suspicious vehicles to search for the missing boy. A witness furnished a composite of a man she saw talking to a boy believed to be Timmy, as well as a suspected vehicle. This information was given to the media in hopes that a citizen might recognize the subject.

Six days after Timmy disappeared, his suffocated body was found along a main street in Wayne County. The killer had broken his pattern and dumped Timmy outside of the county.

The state police crime lab personnel processed the scene and the body apparently revealed no sexual abuse. An autopsy later revealed he had been molested.

Several concerned groups posted rewards totaling $70,000 for the arrest of the child killer. The Task Force was flooded with over 12,000 tips. Parents turned in sons, brothers turned in brothers, and church members turned in their pastors. Realizing the individual agencies could not bear the financial responsibilities of immense investigations, the Task Force was awarded $700,000 to fund and equip 21 investigators for six months to identify and capture the killer.

A computer system was installed to assist the Task Force. Before the computer, several investigators, resulting in a loss of time and duplication of effort, would investigate several tips concerning the same individual. The computer system allowed names of suspects in any of the four homicides to be entered and checked. Working under the theory that the killer was not successful every time he attempted to abduct a child, the Task Force surveyed all area schools. What they found was startling. Over 1,100 cases of attempted abductions were never reported to the police or to the child's parents. The usual reason given by the child, "If Mom knew she wouldn't let me play there anymore."

Although admirable efforts were made at supervision of the 300 investigators, coordination was nearly impossible. It was a case of "too much, too late." Some departments were virtually using the Task Force as a training experience for their personnel. The mere fact that some of the investigators were inexperienced led to the improper elimination of some suspects.

Unfortunately, the notoriety of the investigation received nationwide coverage, and some investigators lost sight of their objectives and placed more emphasis on pleasing the media. They ignored the accepted practice of sometimes withholding information known only to the police and the responsible parties.

Spreen concluded his presentation with a plea for consolidation of law enforcement services.

These cases continued to haunt Spreen through the years. Recently, he was happy to hear from an old friend, Sgt. Garry Gray, currently in charge of the Oakland Child Killer Task Force that an arrest was finally made in 2006.

The arrest of 65 year-old Theodore Lamborgine was announced December 12, 2006. Lamborgine and Richard Lawson, who is in prison for sexual and assault charges against children, were involved in a sex ring together, say reporters. Officials are not sure that Lamborgine is responsible for the murders of the four children in Oakland County but it is the first arrest in the case, which began in 1976-77. He has not admitted killing the children but has admitted raping them, saying that they wanted the relations and saying that he paid them for having sex with him. However, one of Lamborgine's children, Tanner, believes he killed the four children and stated on a website, "May he rot in hell."

Another first instigated by the Sheriff Spreen's Department in 1978 was an Outdoor Warning Program to warn citizens of impending danger by installing outdoor warning sirens. Today the county has 216 total sirens. Spreen also encouraged the formation of the Michigan Deputy Sheriff's Association which formally began in 1978, an organization created for employees of sheriffs' departments. The organization fulfills many needs but top on Spreen's list was training and issues of professionalism.

On January 27, 1979, two men wearing facemasks broke into Great

Scott Supermarket in Farmington and killed a 62-year-old supermarket employee. They wanted money for narcotics, bound the employees, and asked the older man to open the store safe. When he couldn't, they shot him in the head in front of the other horrified employees. The pair then fled with the employees' personal belongings and some cigarettes. William Hess, 18 at the time, and Darrell Kastel, 22 at the time, were friends. They kept in contact for some time after the murder, even serving time together in prison. Investigators of the Oakland County Sheriff's Department reopened the case in 2006, leading to the arrest of the two men after nearly thirty years.

In 1979, alcohol-related traffic crashes were the primary cause of death for people under the age of 40 in Oakland County. During that year, 100 people lost their lives in alcohol-related crashes. To address this serious issue, a countywide Alcohol Enforcement Team was created. They patrolled major roadways in target locations throughout the county that were identified by the Sheriff's Department as having a high volume of alcohol-related motor vehicle crashes. The team was extremely successful in both Operating Under the Influence of Liquor (OUIL) arrests, and community education and awareness. In 1979, before the AE Team began operating, the Oakland County Sheriff's Department made 51 OUIL arrests annually. In the three years of the federal grant, the Sheriff's Department OUIL arrests totaled 2,886, with 59 percent made by the six officers of the AE Team. The Sheriff's Department still operates the Alcohol Enforcement Team.

Many law enforcement pundits heard Sheriff Johannes Spreen's plea for consolidation of services. He was elected the national president of the American Academy for Professional Law Enforcement. He was asked to address the Academy in Chicago on May 17, 1979. He was also the Director of the Center for the Administration of Justice at Mercy College in Detroit. That was part of the reason they invited him to give this talk. His talk was entitled "Law Enforcement Coordination: Is the Sheriff the Key?" His message was that the future sheriff could be a modern "tribune" who can champion the people's rights such as the right to relative peace, safety, and security in an effective law enforcement system at a cost we can afford.

Spreen's ideas gained a foothold in law enforcement thinking. The importance of the American sheriff has grown over the last thirty years. Sheriffs exist now in every state except Alaska and Connecticut. In most states, sheriffs are elected. In Hawaii, the chief justice appoints the sheriffs, while in Rhode Island, the governor appoints sheriffs for each county. In Connecticut, towns were established so early that they never had county government, and they hire or appoint marshals to serve civil papers, transport prisoners, and handle the jails.   M a n y police departments have been disbanded and cities have turned to contracts with the sheriffs' departments to save money on manpower, facilities, communications equipment, investigations, and to run the jails. While that is expensive for a community, it is more expensive for a little town to maintain even a small police force.

On April 19, 1979, Johannes' wife, Elinor, died of multiple sclerosis and complications. He slept in the emergency room for ten of the last eleven days. The doctor told Johannes that he had to perform an emergency operation to remove fluid or something from Elinor's lungs. He thinks it was called a pneumothorax, but it did not help. She passed away that night. He held her hand and said, "I love you." Betty was there at the bedside, too.

Johannes recalled that the doctor's name was Freivogel, which means "free bird" in German. Was he the instrument of freeing Elinor from her debilitating, incapacitating multiple sclerosis? Her death allowed her soul to escape her weakened and tortured body and fly away. All this together with his life experiences made Johannes find it hard to remain an agnostic.

After 31 years of marriage, he and daughter, Betty, were left to manage alone. He filled the emptiness by deciding to run for a third term as sheriff.

Sheriff Spreen in the spring of 1979, running for a third term.

Spreen was asked to give a talk to the first joint meeting between Michigan police chiefs and Michigan sheriffs on June 30, 1981. His ideas on consolidation of law enforcement had continued to proliferate. He told the audience that it was time for police and sheriffs to unite under the common task of meeting challenges. He described how there were 103 police departments that encircle Detroit in the counties of Wayne, Oakland and Macomb. This immense fragmentation was a delight to the criminal mind and a frustration to the sincere police officer and police executive.

Most concerned police executives voluntarily cooperate in spite of the fragmentation. However, there are islands of isolation where there should be bridges of understanding. This was a group all bound to the same common public trust of protection for the citizenry but divided by their lack of trust in each other. This lack of trust is a natural defense that developed in a time of change and financial cutbacks. They become jealous of other chiefs and sheriffs as possible threats. They covet information, rather than share information. However, citizens see the police as one body of people, whether the uniform be brown or blue, cooperating to fight crime and prevent accidents. The public does not understand overlapping and fragmented policing service.

Spreen did not believe in one large county police department but urged agencies to work together to free themselves of the jurisdictional constraints that impede solving crimes. Police should be close to the people they serve. Rapport between the police officer and the citizen is one of the chief defenses in curbing and preventing crime, he argued. However, local police cannot do everything themselves.

Spreen's contribution was to sell various law enforcement agencies on the need to work together, avoid petty turf battles, and to establish coordination to solve crimes of this magnitude. Many counties across the country have now implemented his recommendations.

Innovation 7:
Non-partisan elections for sheriffs

Sheriff Spreen talked with Ed Meese in 1980, who later became attorney general under President Ronald Reagan the following year. During Reagan's presidential campaign, Meese served as chief of staff and senior issues adviser for the Reagan-Bush committee. Talking about the problem of politics and campaigning, Spreen told Meese, "I ran as a Democrat, talked like a Republican and acted like an Independent. It comes at a price to run as a Democrat in a Republican county. The opposition scrutinized my every move and they instigated several investigations during my tenure." Meese sympathized and agreed that sheriff should be a non-partisan position instead of being tied to politics.

Sheriff Johannes Spreen urged the Michigan Sheriff's Association in 1981 to pursue the possibility of non-partisan elections for sheriffs in order to have a better chance to remove politics, factionalism and favoritism that could hinder professional ethics. A sheriff's role is to provide policing where there is no policing, and to provide specialized, scientific assistance to each department within the county.

Spreen set up some programs that dealt specifically with cooperation between local police departments and the sheriff's department. He called one program S.H.A.R.E. (Scientific Homicide, Arson and Rape Effort.) He had the pleasure of deputizing a number of local police officers that completed 40 hours of training in homicide investigation, and then had a team prepared to investigate any major homicide in a participating jurisdiction in Oakland County.

He instituted a program through the Oakland Community College Police Academy whereby data was compiled comprehensively on all arsons that occurred in the county. Members of the Sheriff's Department Arson Unit, members of the Southfield and Troy Police Departments and other agencies worked together on major investigations and data sharing. He commented,

These types of sharing concepts are only the beginning. Other services of a sheriff's department could and should provide local jurisdictions with specialized traffic programs, accident reconstruction, police driver training and other activities. Other supportive services could include crime lab services, a comprehensive juvenile delinquency prevention program, marine program, canine, and various types of specialized training and aviation services. Common dilemmas require immediate joint action to succeed. Continuing on divisive paths invite efficiency experts to force agencies to do that which we could do on our own: cooperate.

Spreen's plea and pressure was heard by other states. Since then, the following states have considered or have permitted the election of non-partisan sheriffs: Florida, Oregon, Georgia, Washington, Louisiana, Nevada, Oklahoma, and Montana.

INNOVATION 8:
Sheriff's scooter officers in townships

In 1982, Sheriff Spreen was the only sheriff in America success-fully using scooters in townships. Spreen always pushed the concept of community service officers with two-wheeled scooters to handle many calls, foster people-police rapport and to leave the patrol cars ready and available for serious emergency type runs. Scooter teams were not in competition with patrol cars but worked in harmony and rapport with them. His concept of dual policing was to stress prevention of crime as well as enforcement of laws in police work. However, it took him years to gain support for this concept.

He had to battle for this because many police officers felt the pre-vention (community policing) was soft on crime or wasn't "real" police work. Many sergeants and lieutenants resisted allowing cops to devise their own solutions for community problems, fearing a loss of control. Even as late as 1983, the *Detroit News* quoted Spreen saying, "We've got a lot of officers out there who feel their job is nothing but 'shoot—chase—shoot—chase.' Their job as a social scientist and all the good they can do has somehow eluded them."

He funded the scooters in the sheriff's program by enlisting people to sell hot dogs and beer at the Pontiac Silverdome. With 150 volun-teers, they also sold the game programs at Superbowl 16, setting the record by selling $19,000 of programs in one day—the most that had ever been sold. He had help from volunteers in Explorer Scouts, Re-serves, and a program called ESCAPE (Enroll in Sheriff's Crime and Accident Prevention and Education) and Shriners.

Sheriff's posse of Shriners around 1980.

Volunteers worked at Elias Brothers Restaurant to raise money for the ESCAPE program in 1981. Spreen's wife, Mona, is next to him.

Selling hotdogs and popcorn at the Silverdome with Deputy Marc Cooper as McGruff the Crime Dog and Kelly, Mona's daughter.

In 1980, Spreen decided to run for Governor the following year. He had to get 18,000 signatures. Republican candidates only had to get 9,000. It's always tough to unseat an incumbent governor, especially one as popular as Republican Gov. William Milliken. He wrote the letter below to 83 county sheriffs in Michigan to acquire enough names on petitions to get on the ballot as a candidate for Michigan governor.

Dear Sheriff:

I have always been dedicated to law enforcement, and in the last six years particularly to the very important role of the Sheriff. I see the Sheriff as the key and the hope for cooperative law enforcement in the future.

I am running, as I hope you know, for Governor on the Democratic ticket. While you may have another commitment or preference at this time, I am especially asking you to help at least get me on the ballot.

I promise to speak out for all Sheriffs' departments and for proper cooperative law enforcement in general, as a very important factor in the quality of life in Michigan. With a background of 37 years in law enforcement, mostly with city police departments in New York and Detroit, I have developed the greatest respect for the vital role of the office of Sheriff.

Please give me the opportunity to at least speak out on issues important to you and to Michigan—and I would like to hear from you on these.

Enclosed please find a number of petitions, and I would ask for at least 150 signatures through your good offices. If you can get 1,000—all the better. I need your help. Our deadline for petitions is June 6, therefore we would like to have them all in by June 1.

Thank you.

Sincerely, Johannes F. Spreen

He lost out getting on the ballot by 108 signatures by the deadline. Republican Governor William Milliken was re-elected for a third term but laws passed since then prevent a governor being re-elected for a third term.

Spreen was honored to make a presentation at the 1980 Society of Automobile Engineers (SAE) Congress and Exposition in Detroit on February 27, 1980. He decided to try to describe the life of law enforcement officers so they could appreciate the profession better. Here are some of the things he told them.

In law enforcement, the work environment is extremely

critical because it is often unstable and constantly changing. Being a law enforcement officer is dangerous, and the mental stress and fatigue of facing unknown danger day after day, year after year, builds up protective barriers. Can you imagine the tension faced by the officer during every traffic stop, family fight, neighbor dispute, not knowing if one of these people will try to take his life? More police officers are killed each year handling these types of calls than during armed robberies or burglaries.

The whole role of police officers has changed for the last decade. A police officer is no longer just a guardian of the peace. He must be a sociologist, psychologist, lawyer, physician, marriage counselor, educator, and babysitter. Compounding this, the public's attitude towards police officers has changed, and as a result, there has been a corresponding loss of respect for law enforcement and for laws in general. This loss of respect sometimes develops into open hostility against the officers themselves. Besides the physical injury that often accompanies this hostility, it may lead to high frustration levels in the police officers.

Many officers give up high paying jobs or go right from college into the law enforcement profession because they have a desire to serve their community and help their fellow man. Many look at it as a "calling," a service to others that most citizens are reluctant to accept. Law enforcement is considered useful —as long as it doesn't touch the individual person. It's all right for the other guy to get the ticket or be arrested for drunk driving, but if it ever happens to us, then the cop was out to get us.

Home life problems also affect the work environment of the law enforcement officer. The work hours and rotating shifts play havoc on his home life. There are late calls, emergencies, night shifts, and the never-ending court appearances. Marital problems start to surface because the spouse begins to demand that the officer spend more time at home.

A police officer can't just forget about work when he's done for a day. He's on duty 24 hours a day and no matter where he may be, he must be ready to enforce the law and to protect citizens. A physician may choose to respond to an emergency as he drives past a wreck on the street, whereas a police officer is required by law to stop and render service even if he's off-duty.

Because he deals with criminals constantly and also the problems of society, the police officer may develop a cynical attitude towards life and the public. Police officers feel that their hands are tied by liberal court decisions giving the criminals more of a break and little or no restitution to the victims of the crimes. Weeks of work put into solving a crime may go out the window because of some legal mistake the officer was not trained to recognize. Incompetent and lenient judges continually release criminals and lower bonds allowing dangerous criminals freedom once again to ravage the streets of our communities.

As in other fields, alcoholism, divorce, extra-marital affairs, and sometimes suicide are the emotional releases upon which a few frustrated police officers come to rely.

A police officer often feels isolated, not only from the community and management, but from other police officers in other neighboring communities. There is little coordinated police action across jurisdictional boundary lines and each community becomes like an island in a sea of surging crime. Lack of coordination between detective bureaus in major criminal cases often causes vital clues and information to be overlooked or never seen at all.

Part of the problem is that many have felt lost in the administrative shuffles. Their attitudes have been shaped because they feel they have no say in problem-solving or management operations. The Oakland County Sheriff's Department is now operating a new concept of team policing. Each member of the team is trained as a specialist in a particular area of interest and the members are working together as a unit. Cross-fertilization occurs as each trains the other in his unique specialty. The organizational rank structure is eliminated and direct communication between top management and team members now takes place weekly. I am an active participant with the three teams that have been established.

They are encouraged to make suggestions for new operational procedures and to experiment with new techniques in police operations. To make this new organization work, we are now in your communities listening to your problems, talking to you on a one to one basis, and working together to solve the problems with the people and their law enforcement agencies.

Our department is now using contract law enforcement services. We have developed a service that allows small communities or large townships to contract for police protection from our department. Under this agreement, we assign a specific number of officers to patrol that community. The community also has the back-up support services of investigators, crime lab, aviation, marine division, and administrative staff services.

Most of our officers are selected to serve in those communities in which they reside. This gives each officer a pride in his community because he and his family live there. Substations have been established in communities, which give officers a centralized location within the community to which they can report for work. This has eliminated the officer driving many miles out of his way just to fulfill manpower requirements.

One of our major problems was shift preference; and, working closely with the officers' union representatives, we reached an agreement to solve this problem. We now give officers the choice of selecting first and second preference of work shifts that best fit his home life pattern. This was important because constant shift changes were found to be highly disruptive for the officers' private lives.

Marital strife is highly prevalent in police work. Quite often the spouse has no idea what the officer does and the stress and problems that he faces daily. Our department is involved in an awareness program for the wives, which gives them a full orientation including the opportunity to go on patrol with their husbands to see exactly how they work. Tonight I will welcome the spouses of our corrections officers and walk them through the jail blocks to gain a perspective into what it's like on both sides of the bars.

To further improve the environment in which the officer operates, we are fostering more citizen involvement through educational programs to explain laws and the criminal justice system, and to become crime prevention conscious. I have entitled this program ESCAPE, which is an acronym for "*E*nlisted in the *S*heriffs *C*rime and *A*ccident *P*revention *E*ducation" program.

I have outlined to you some of the programs our Sheriff's Department is implementing in an effort to help correct some imperfections. These programs are aimed towards bringing the community and its law enforcement agencies closer together in a true teamwork effort by improving the quality of life in the community and for the officer who serves that community.

Spreen received a letter in April 1981 that said, "This is the last letter you will receive from me Spreen. So get your deputies, judges and the prosecutors together, because I am going to kill you all."

On May 3, 1981, a man nearly killed Sheriff Spreen. A Pontiac man carrying a Bible, a caliber rifle and 200 rounds of ammunition was overpowered Friday by two sheriff's deputies on the Oakland County Courthouse lawn. Police identified the man as Louis Grousnick, who was released six months earlier from the Center for Forensic Psychiatry in Ypsilanti. Authorities said Grousnick had a long history of arrests on charges ranging from firearms to assault and death threats.

Not only were there mentally disturbed people outside the jail, but inside. Spreen said, "It is clear that we must address mental health problems. Most of the mentally ill coming into our jail must be retained in order to protect the public."

In 1980 in Oakland County, the psychiatric team conducted 888 reviews. This was a 46% increase in the persons requiring mental health intervention when compared against 1979. Early in 1981, a 25% increase in mental health requirements of the jailed population required reworking the psychiatric team. He then employed a psychiatric team of five for a correctional system, which houses 650 people per day or more. The system of service delivery includes close coordination of Spreen's department and the psychiatric team provided through the

Oakland County Community Mental Health Department. In addition, essential to this system is the direct support provided through community mental health professionals. The system, which they designed, serves the following purposes:

1. The prompt and accurate identification of mental illness in the jail.
2. Immediate response to mental and emotional crises.
3. Appropriate and comprehensive referral.
4. Appropriate treatment.
5. Time review and monitoring of treatment and behavior.
6. Information sharing.

Spreen's department did not innovate, but they built a reputation for having an excellent triage system for mentally ill people. Gail M. Barton, Rohn S. Friedman, 1986, Haworth Press, cited it in *Handbook of Emergency Psychiatry for Clinical Administrators*. On page 273, the authors wrote:

> An excellent, comprehensive program was developed in Oakland County, Michigan, under the auspices of Johannes F. Spreen, Sheriff. Through the program set up by Sheriff Spreen, the services provided assessment and hospitalization for those in need.

INNOVATION 9:
United police chiefs and sheriffs

On June 30, 1981, Spreen addressed the Michigan Sheriff's Association and the Michigan Chiefs of Police. This was historic because it was the first time that all sheriffs and chiefs in Michigan met in a joint conference.

Spreen was selected because he had been a police chief (commissioner) and was currently a sheriff. However, he felt changes were needed to work together and effectively reduce crime and costs.

At that time, only a few places had consolidated sheriff and police facilities. One of the first consolidations was in Parker County and Weatherford, Texas, where a single building for the records system and booking procedures of sheriff and police was recommended back in 1972. Some places like Indianapolis and Marion County, Indiana, entered into a unified government plan in 1971 but never consolidated police and sheriff departments despite favorable public opinion polls. This wasn't an easy plan or talk to prepare.

> I see before me a group all bound to the same common public trust of protection for the citizenry. Everyone here wished to protect not only his career, but also the people he is sworn to protect. We are gathered together but we are divided by our lack of trust for each other.
>
> This lack of trust is a natural defense that we, as administrators, have developed in a time of change and financial cutbacks. We all sense that changes are imminent, that overlapping and fragmented services face elimination, and consolidation efforts could eliminate our positions. We become jealous of our positions, and we see other chief and sheriffs as possible threats. We covet information, rather than share information. We become further fragmented, rather than united.

We are a group that, when viewed by the public, represents a unified body of law enforcement personnel. A citizen sees the police as one body of people (whether the uniform be brown or blue) cooperating, fighting crime and preventing accidents.

I am here today to ask that we all work together to see that each policing agency secures a role in this mosaic. The public does not understand overlapping and fragmented policing services. By remaining fragmented and competing, not cooperating, we are setting the stage for our own extinction.

If we work together to free ourselves of the jurisdictional, budgetary, and manpower constraints that impede solving crimes (such as arson, auto thefts, and homicides like the child killer), then do we not invite consolidation by another hand? How long can crime outstrip our abilities before county, state, or local governments step in with consolidation programs that we have no hand in?

We must not allow the erosion of trust between agencies to continue. We need trust to be effective, to share information, and make the best use of our scarce manpower. Nothing remains static; we must work to fight distrust lest it become more pervasive and divisive.

The co-ed murders in Michigan some years ago, the child-killer investigations, both in Oakland County and now in Atlanta, and the Jimmy Hoffa disappearance are striking examples of unpreparedness for large scale, multi-jurisdictional investigations.

There ought to be a shared-power concept, a shared-responsibility concept with the sheriff providing certain law enforcement functions of a type that could not be provided as economically and effectively at the municipal or small department level.

It is my firm belief that we must have proper role definition in the State of Michigan. The State police have a very important job to do and that job transcends highway patrol, although I believe they should patrol the major freeways and highways of this state. They should also be heavily into control of the narcotic traffic, control of white-collar crime, certainly into heavy lab and identification assistance to local and county departments.

That may be where the progressive sheriff comes in. The modern sheriff should not carry the burden of a partisan political label. I have asked the Michigan Sheriff's Association to pursue the possibility of non-partisan elections for sheriffs in order to have a better chance to deal with the problems of law enforcement by removing the politics, factionalism, and possible favoritism that could hinder professional ethics.

The sheriff's role should be that of specialized, scientific assistance to the individual community, usurping no department's authority, and threatening no department's sovereignty. A sheriff's role is to provide policing where there is no policing, and to provide supportive assistance to each department within the county.

We have instituted some programs in Oakland County dealing with cooperation between local police departments and the sheriff's department. We call one program S.H.A.R.E. (Scientific Homicide, Arson, and Rape Effort). I recently deputized a number of local police officers who completed 40 hours of training in homicide investigation, and we now have a team prepared to investigate any major homicide in a participating jurisdiction in Oakland County.

Oakland County has a comprehensive countywide arson program. Through the Oakland Community College Police Academy, data is compiled on all arsons which occur within the county. Members of the Sheriff's Arson Unit, several members of local police departments and other local agencies work together on major investigations and the sharing of data.

Our county and cities have entered into a contract whereby the cities pay the salaries of five sergeants whereby professional correction services are provided to the city at the city's jail. This has been mutually satisfactory.

For the last six years, we have provided prisoner transport for all departments within the county to and from the county jail. This takes the burden off the local department, freeing manpower for protective patrol in their own communities.

For many years, Oakland County has been sharing effort and resources in our Narcotics Enforcement Team (NET) operation. Here, State police and local cooperation is exemplified to fight narcotics proliferation among our young people and our schools.

I feel that the modern sheriff's department could and should provide to local jurisdictions specialized traffic programs, accident reconstruction, police driver training, and other programs.

We have a pilot program whereby members of the Michigan State Police, local police departments, and the Sheriff's Department work as a team five nights a week in a concentrated alcohol enforcement program. We have the first mobile breathalyzer operation in the state. Such a program couldn't have gotten off the ground without the effort of all agencies involved.

Other supportive services could include crime lab services, a comprehensive juvenile delinquency prevention program, marine program, canine, and other types of specialized training and aviation services.

I see before me a group of professionals, a brain trust, capable of waging a protracted conflict or coming together to solve our current problems. To fail to coordinate is to fail to progress.

Let us pull together for progress, or continue on divisive paths and fall victim to the consolidation efforts of efficiency experts that will do for us what we should do on our own.

Since then, there have been many efforts to reduce fragmentation and to consolidate sheriff and police departments. Some were Jacksonville, Florida; and Tongue River, Illinois. St. Paul, Minnesota, and Ramsey County co-located a police and sheriff facility. The Pueblo, Colorado, City Council rejected a proposal to combine police and sheriff dispatch centers in 1992 but in 1994, Colorado was studying consolidation for Denver. Sarpy County, Nebraska, conducted a feasibility study for consolidating in 2006.

Johannes' Third Marriage

Spreen's secretary and new undersheriff Robert Nyovich were having a romance in late 1981; despite the fact the Nyovich was married. They concocted a press release about Spreen's wife, Mona Hemmerling, whom widowed Johannes had married in 1980. Spreen decided to fire both parties who had created the press release but his marriage to Mona suffered and they divorced after a short marriage.

Mona was part owner of a tavern in Detroit, and her name was among those mentioned in a 1979 state police report of a booze smuggling investigation involving customs. Spreen said that "was the beginning of the end of my short marriage to the ever secretive and mysterious Mona Jo Hemmerling, whom I divorced later."

The 1979 Michigan State Police report named her as part owner of a Detroit bar that was suspected of selling smuggled liquor. Commissioner James Lanni, R-Royal Oaks asked the county's Organized Crime Unit to investigate "possible improprieties" in the sheriff's department saying that there are "many questions about activities" in the department. However, when pressed to name them, Lanni did not mention the controversial intelligence report, which he said he had not seen. Instead, he said the finance committee of the Board of Commissioners planned to "go over an audit of the sheriff's gasoline supply."

James Lanni continued his accusations about Spreen. No sooner would one thing get resolved than Lanni would bring up something else, each requiring unnecessary audits. Typically, the newspaper reports findings at the completion of the audit such as this one.

Sandra Combs of *The Oakland Press* did a story on April 23, 1982 called "Audit Clears Spreen of State Funds Misuse."

> Michigan's auditor general has found no basis for charges of misuse of state grant funds by the Oakland County Sheriff's Department.
>
> The audit was conducted after allegations were lodged against the department in December 1981 concerning the use of Secondary Road Patrol grant funds. The funds totaled about $350,000 annually in 1979, 1980 and 1981. It quoted Inspector Lee saying, "Our review did not disclose misuse of SRP

grant funds for the allegations regarding the clerk position and the supplanting of (those) funds for county funds through reassignment of sergeants."

Years later, Spreen said, of James Lanni, "I feel he was one of the worst, most vicious politicians I have ever encountered. Now he is a registered sex offender. Yes, what goes around, comes around."

By March of 1983, Mona, the thin, attractive 39-year-old wife of 63-year-old Johannes Spreen was attracting more negative media attention for selling smuggled liquor from Canada, having alleged private liaisons with known organized-crime figures and possible hidden ownership of her bar-restaurant by known crime figures. She told one reporter that her biggest regret was not having told Spreen immediately about a $15,000 loan. "I didn't tell him because I wanted to protect our relationship," she said.

At the twilight of Johannes career as sheriff, for the first time in his life, he was receiving negative media attention mainly because of his wife.

Mona and Johannes separated shortly. He was bitterly upset by her lies but Mona and Johannes still had (and still have) great regard for each other. It was hard for Johannes to end the relationship, which had been good for Mona's daughter. They continued to communicate with each other despite the separation.

One other important event of Spreen's term occurred in 1983. The Oakland County Sheriff's Department went on record as not providing free patrolling of communities unless they were paid and contracted to provide such services. To this day, spokesmen such as Mike McCabe for that Sheriff's office say, "We don't provide free patrols to any community." Without funds, no agency can provide services. This precedent set by Spreen continues to be cited in counties as they argue the pros and cons of small communities desiring police presence without wanting to pay for a police force.

CHAPTER SEVEN:
Sallie: Johannes' Fourth Wife)

In 1984, Sallie Rose Highstreet was working for the Council on Aging as Program Coordination. It was a very sad time for her. Her divorce from her husband, George Highstreet, of 33 years was to be final in a month, when she took her walking group to the Senior Olympics in Farmington Hills.

They were having lunch in the cafeteria at the college and dancing to the band that was playing when this handsome stranger came up to them and said he was the sheriff. They were all wearing T-shirts that said "Senior Street Walker." The man who claimed to be sheriff said, "I think I'll have to run you girls in, but the jail is full. Just have a picture taken with me and I'll let you go."

Sallie said, "Well, I made him show his badge. Then we took the picture. I sent him the picture. I thought mmmm-not bad, but he's probably married."

The next year, Sallie's group went to the Senior Olympics again—same shirts—"Senior Street Walkers." Sallie wasn't quite a senior yet but it was her group of seniors and she took them walking. There he was again. This year he was getting a divorce. This time he had entered the Senior Olympic race-walk and Sallie was at the finish line waiting for her seniors. Spreen won the race, came up to Sallie and said, "What does your husband think about you wearing a shirt like that?"

She said, "I don't have a husband," batting her eyes and smiling.

He said, "Would you like to have dinner with me some time."

Shy person that she was, she said, "Yeah!"

She was doing a Late Life Divorce Support Group at that time and he called for a date. She wasn't available that time but when he heard she was doing the support group for divorcees, he said, "Boy, do I need you."

On October 12, 1985, Sallie made this note. "Had my second date with Johannes. He is someone I could care about. He is so interesting because he has done so much. He is a great dancer (it seems so good to dance again) and he is TALL. I love it. He is going through divorce so he is hurting—must go slow—no more hurts for me and he does not need any more, either."

They met every Saturday night at Surf North, living 67 miles apart. He would drive all that way and they would meet. Sallie was smart. She chose a place that had dancing. They had a nice dinner, a little wine, danced, and she would listen to him. They became friends. She had been through divorce and knew how hard it was. She said to a friend, "I really admire this man. He is a good honorable man but he is so sad. I could never be serious about anyone without a sense of humor."

Well, the dancing got closer—the smiles started to come—and then laughter. Finally, after six months of dating, he still had not kissed her—so she kissed him.

When Sallie's grandson, Jay, met Johannes the first time, he said, "Are you going to marry my grandma?" He then tried to warn his future grandpa of his grandmother's serious flaw. "Have you seen her pitch-white legs?" Little Jay didn't know that pitch was black and they were amused by his comment.

Before Johannes and Sallie married, she convinced him to do a series of talks for her seniors along with her. They were entitled "Mind, Body, and Spirit." Sallie said, "In high school, they give a Spirit Award not necessarily to the best athlete but to the person that keeps everyone's spirit up—the one with the most enthusiasm. By the way," she added, "enthusiasm means God within. In life, it is its own reward. Enthusiasm is the foundation for a winning attitude."

Johannes was touched as he heard her speak and watched her helping others. Johannes finally proposed to Sallie on his knees, offering a box of chocolates with a diamond ring embedded in the center chocolate.

After three years of delightful courtship, he married Sallie on December 28, 1988. As she said, "I married Mr. Right. I just didn't know his first name was Always!" ("Well, he is mostly!")

At their wedding, Sallie's three sons gave her away and Johannes' daughter, Betty, gave him away. After the marriage, Sallie and Johannes set off on a honeymoon cruise.

Over a year later, they traveled to Germany to visit Johannes' birthplace. Here are some of Sallie's recollections.

Hildesheim, Germany: It was in the month of May in 1990. I know that because of the wonderful white asparagus (frische spargel) we ate all over Germany. It was my first trip to Germany. We stayed in a beautiful hotel—Hotel Forte. Our window opened onto the market square. We watched all the excitement from our window—sitting on the windowsill. They were celebrating 500 years of the German Post (the mail). We danced in our room as the band played the German waltzes. (Johannes stepped on my hearing aid. Good news was it was not in my ear at the time.)

We watched the French Open Tennis Tournament on TV—a French happening with a German commentator—a real experience.

On Saturday, the market place was filled with farmers bringing in their wares—flowers, vegetables, fruit, cheese, and great bratwurst. Oh, yes, we had some of that—served with a small piece of dark bread and mustard—so good!

I love the German breakfast but the buffet at this hotel was the very best. Beautiful fruit, cheeses, ever-present boiled eggs, granola, yogurt, and those delicious rolls and meats. It was wonderful tasting and beautifully served with China plates, cloth napkins, and flowers on the tables.

We had a lovely tea set in our room with cookies. We would have our tea as we looked out the window watching the lives of the Germans.

The best food I ever ate was here in Hildesheim, sitting in an outdoor café by our hotel. We had white asparagus and potatoes covered with a white sauce or gravy, and Rote Griitze, a raspberry dessert. It was the best dessert I ever tasted. I've never found anything to match it any place else. What a lovely memory.

Johannes and Sallie in his hometown at a beautiful
restaurant in Osterholz-Scharmbeck, Germany.

Sallie has many other memories of Johannes, which reveal other
sides of this "legendary lawman." Here are some of the things she has
written about him over the years since they married.

> My husband, Johannes, has sent me many beautiful and
> romantic cards. I have them all. The other afternoon I got the
> mail and there was a letter for me from my honey. What a sur-
> prise, because he was sitting across from me at the table reading
> the paper. I laughed and said, "Hey, I just received a letter from
> you." He smiled and continued to read the paper. I opened the
> letter and to my surprise, it was a couple of pages of wonderful
> words telling me how much I mean to him. Wow! Again—
> tears, happy tears.
>
> A Chinese proverb says, "You cannot give a rose to some-
> one without some of the fragrance remaining on your hand."

It was her 63rd birthday on January 30, 1994. Johannes said, "Pack
a bag and be prepared for anything." In the five years since they married, each birthday surprise was better than the year before. Wow!
What wonderful thing had he planned for this year, she wondered. She
wrote:

> My heart fell when he started talking about some tent city

in the desert. He explained with excitement in his voice, "I talked to Sheriff Joe Arpaio and he is experimenting with tents for the prisoners. It's a cheaper way to incarcerate and he will allow and even encourages citizens to come visit and spent the night to check it out. And it only costs $25 a person."

Oh, yeah. Just what I always wanted to do. Spend the night with a bunch of criminals in a tent in the desert with all the creepy crawlies—slimy individuals and critters. And we had to pay for it. My fear of snakes is unreal. I knew I wouldn't sleep a wink in that environment.

I couldn't tell John how I felt. He was so thrilled with this new and different surprise for me. Oh, well. I'd survive. So I didn't let the disappointment show in my face or be heard in my voice. But ugh! Yuck!

He drove to Scottsdale, passed the Princess Hotel (that would have been nice). It was getting more deserty all the time. I was sure the snakes were all banding together to attack me as soon as we arrived at this tent city, wherever it was.

John rattled on. "Oh, these tents are supposed to be very nice. This will be a real experience. You will love seeing how nice the prisoners are treated." Yeah, right!

"Oh, wait," he said. "I think I've gone too far. It's supposed to be on a ranch." He turned around and went back past the Princess, back into civilization. He pulled into the regal Mc-Cormick Ranch where he explained there would be a meeting before we were assigned to our tent.

The meeting was in Room 345. Strange to have it on the third floor. He opened the door. No meeting, a lovely room, no tent! A wonderful birthday. Dining, tennis, meeting old friends, shopping, and sleeping in a real bed—and not one slimy creepy critter to be found. He did it again. A super birthday.

My husband gives to me every day. After being married for 33 years to a very selfish and uncaring man, it is so wonderful to bask in the loveliness of living with Johannes, my husband.

Johannes and Sallie on an Alaskan cruise in 1995.

We start every day with a hug—that comes before the coffee he has made for me and the paper he places by my coffee cup at the breakfast table. He would make my breakfast for me if I wanted it. I'm not a breakfast eater or a morning person. After coffee and reading the paper, we talk. He values my opinion. He makes me feel like "somebody," compliments me on most everything I do, or how I look when dressed up.

He encourages me to take classes, and to play tennis. (Old what's his name—my former husband—told me to hit the wall—tennis term for hitting the ball up against a solid wood green backboard that returns the ball to you—you play alone. Old what's his name didn't want to play with me.)

Johannes loves to surprise me with special gifts, trips, cards or notes. He is the one that massages my poor feet when I've had a hard day.

He is my friend, my companion, my soul mate.

Recently Sallie wrote,

Now that I am old, my favorite thing to do is sit out on our dock and watch the freighters go by. Ships from all over the world pass our house on the St. Clair River. My husband,

Johannes, a New York kid, says, "You see one freighter, you've seen them all." Yet, I watch him taking pictures and trying to read the names and where they are from. He doesn't fool me. He loves them, too.

St. Clair River behind the Spreen's Michigan home.

I love gifts. My husband, Johannes, has given me so many wonderful gifts—diamonds, jewelry, great things, and I love getting them. But they pale in the gift of himself he has given me—his support, compassion, understanding, his love.

Johannes encouraged Sallie to enter the 1999 Ms. Senior Michigan Pageant and she won and became Ms. Senior Michigan.

Sallie Spreen, Ms. Senior Michigan, 1999.

Johannes and Sallie entered a new era of their lives after joining the Toastmasters' International Club. They created skits to entertain senior citizens in Michigan and Arizona. Their second career as entertainers included impersonations of many celebrities including W. C. Fields and Mae West.

W. C. Fields and Mae West

After several years of entertaining citizens in Michigan, they received the 1999 St. Clair County Council on Aging award as "Outstanding Senior Citizens." It was the first time the award was ever given
to a couple.

Outstanding Senior Citizens of 1999 Award
in St. Clair County, Michigan.

CHAPTER EIGHT:
Spreen's Last Election

Let us return to the end of Johannes Spreen's professional life near the end of his last term as Oakland County Sheriff. As Spreen told some reporters in May 1984, "I don't know whether to run for re-election as sheriff, or for county executive, or run for cover."

On June 2, 1984, he entered the race for county executive. He intended to oppose current incumbent Daniel T. Murphy and one of his former Sheriff's Department captains, Bill Nolin, in a six-man race. He promised, if elected, to cut the executive's "excessive" $76,665-a-year salary by 10 percent. Spreen said, "No county executive should make more than the governor." His pay as sheriff was $48,000 per year, and he collected a New York police pension of $13,000.

June 7, 1984, Tom Walsh, editor of the *Detroit Free Press*, wrote a column called, "Don't Count the Sheriff Out."

> Leave it to Oakland's maverick sheriff, Johannes Spreen, to breathe some life into an otherwise ho-hum election campaign for county offices...
>
> He filed to run for county executive against Murphy, a gamble no other big-name Democrat was willing to take...
>
> With President Reagan heading the ticket, and Michigan Democrats saddled with fallout from the state income tax hike, 1984 is widely viewed as a can't-miss year for the GOP...
>
> The man does have Name Recognition, capital letters intended. With the exception of Patterson, no politician in the county has a higher profile than Spreen.

Murphy doesn't come close. A low-key guy who rarely calls a press conference, Murphy's reputation as a sound fiscal administrator springs partly from shunning things like chauffeur-driven limousines and other trappings of the politically powerful that are commonplace in a nearby city that begins with D. For the record, Spreen drives himself to work, too.

Another plus for Spreen is that he's good on the airwaves. At 6'4", he's an imposing television figure. He speaks well and oozes sincerity. [As Spreen said, "Dammit, I am sincere!"] Often in politics, delivering the message with authority is as important as the message itself.

Spreen received much support by citizens and colleagues. An example is this letter from Dennis M. Aaron, Oakland County Commissioner for Oak Park, published June 17, 1984, in the letter to the editor section of the *Detroit News.* It was entitled "A Vote for Spreen."

> For 12 years, I have watched County Executive Murphy and his Republican-controlled board of commissioners systematically destroy Sheriff Spreen's efforts toward better law enforcement and better jail management.
>
> Under Mr. Murphy's leadership, staffing the jail was reduced below nationally recognized standards. The sheriff's pleas for more jailers and for increased jail capacity went unheeded. Finally, the Federal Court in Detroit interceded and ordered Oakland County to do what the sheriff had been asking for over the years. Murphy's indifference to the problems at the jail, unfortunately, results in the taxpayers paying for his poor judgment.
>
> Millions have been wasted over the years in grandiose political schemes. Food disappears from county-managed cafeterias, meaningless jobs done by the administrative staff are constantly being added to the budget, contracts are awarded to the "high bidders" instead of to "low bidders"—and *The News* remains silent, ignoring obvious waste and management on the part of Oakland County Executive Murphy.
>
> I have watched my fellow Republican commissioners abdi-

cate their responsibilities and simply vote the way that Murphy wants them to vote. The Murphy machine may be good politics for him, but it is bad government for Oakland County.

Yes, I think that a change is needed in Oakland County and I am proud to cast a vote for "Spreen."

Dennis M. Aaron, Oakland County Commissioner, Oak Park.

Spreen lost the election for County Executive to Daniel Murphy. He finished his term as sheriff and retired.

CHAPTER NINE:
Retirement

In his retirement, Johannes Spreen often gives talks. He writes articles and books, and teaches many groups. He has numerous interactions in various clubs and activities with old friends and new friends. People still write about him from time to time.

In 1994, Spreen was interviewed about senior citizens in Cherry Beach.

"You seem so dedicated to senior fitness. Did that come with your retirement?"

No, I have always been pretty active, always been a tennis player and I used to run a lot. But I never was a swimmer. Now I'm winning medals for the backstroke in the senior Olympics. And I do walk three miles every morning.

"At what point did you start teaching the aging courses?"

That was after I met Sallie. She was program coordinator for the St. Clair Council on Aging and started many of the programs at Cherry Beach Center. I teach the Body Recall class there three times a week in the summer.

"Is Body Recall an exercise course?"

Yes. We usually exercise for 30 minutes and then do a routine that I designed. It's to the music from the show "Cats." Body Recall is good for me. The body is a movement machine and you have to keep working at it and walking and swimming.

"What kind of classes do you teach in Arizona?"

We embrace a curriculum called Positive Attitudes for Positive Aging. Beyond the fitness, we teach coping skills and memory improvement courses. This October we will be teaching round dancing and I will teach conversational German.

"The memory course sounds interesting. What's it all about?"

I read a lot of self-help books and I've read a lot on the brain and memory. The books talk about how everything we do and hope to ever do is right up there.

"Do you miss being in uniform at all?"

I miss it in a way but I'm too old now.

"You sound to be in pretty good shape."

Well, I'm alive and enjoying life. We aren't going to let old age hamper us and we're getting a chance to help others.

Spreen became involved with Toastmasters International several years ago. Sallie reluctantly joined Toastmasters at Johannes' prodding. She made her second speech entitled, "Old Is Not Bad." She later cut this six and one-half minute award-winning address to two minutes, 45 seconds to become Mrs. Senior Michigan 1999. She also placed in the top ten for Mrs. Senior America and discovered speech was her talent.

Johannes submitted an article about Toastmasters International, which he and wife Sallie totally enjoyed. Here are some excerpts from his article in the *Times Herald* of Port Huron, Michigan, on September 13, 2000.

Do you want to change the world? Do you want to change the course of history? Then learn to speak well. Learn to speak with passion. Speak with feeling on what you believe! Join Toastmasters.

Toastmasters teach that how we speak sends a powerful message. When we speak, people receive impressions for better or for worse. The spoken word can persuade.

Let me share this quote with you: "All great world-shaking events have been brought about not by written matter but by the spoken word."

Jesus Christ did not write anything. Consider and reflect: "The only thing we have to fear is fear itself." Franklin D. Roosevelt. "Ask not what your country can do for you but what you can do for your country!" John F. Kennedy. "Mr. Gorbachev, tear down this wall." Ronald Reagan.

Toastmasters helps us speak better, use gestures to good effect, use proper rate, pitch and tone of voice, and the importance of effective eye contact.

Friends, strangers, employers judge you by your speech. And as you see, there is power of persuasion by the power of your speech. You might not shape the world, but you can change the course of history—your history!

For information on joining a Toastmasters club near your home or business, call Toastmasters International, (800) 9-WE-SPEAK or locally at (800) 96TOAST.

A Michigan newspaper reporter wrote this story on July 10, 2003, about Spreen called "Big Fellow Spreen Has What It Takes to Be a Great Police Officer."

It's been more than five years now since the "Big Fellow" and I competed against each other in a race-walking contest at Port Huron High School's track and field area.

The walk-off took place during an early spring St. Clair County Senior Citizen Olympic meet. If memory serves me right, I was 63 and the "Big Fellow," 6-foot-5-inch Johannes F. Spreen of Marine City, was 78. There were eight of us senior citizens (55 years and older) in that race.

That beautiful senior citizen Olympic moment was recalled for me recently when I received a letter and book from Johannes who said: "John, I remember well that nip-and-tuck race we had a few years ago."

Johannes is affectionately called the "Big Fellow" because of his height, his extraordinary athletic prowess and stamina, and for being an octogenarian. He is 83 now, and there are few in his competitive age bracket that can hold a candle to this incredible force.

In 1985, Johannes retired from a career in law enforcement that spanned nearly 45 years. He was a role model for police officers across the country. His enthusiasm, wit, and literary brilliance continue to shine as a beacon of light for everyone. And who would have thought that this one-time beat patrol officer would one day help to restructure the New York City Police Academy training to a college program. The academy, a West Point for officers, is now John Jay College for Criminal Justice.

Where did Johannes Spreen come from, this gifted person who became a college professor and newspaper columnist after taking his talent from New York to Detroit as police commissioner and later as sheriff of Oakland County?

He was born in Germany, Sept. 28, 1919, in a village outside the city of Bremen. He arrived in New York in 1923 aboard the ocean liner *S.S. Seydlitz* with his mother and sister. They joined his father and brother and settled in Brooklyn. The rest is a matter of record.

Johannes has a bachelor's, master's, and doctorate (all but his dissertation) degrees in law enforcement. He served as a lieutenant bombardier in the Army Air Corps during World War II.

He rose through the ranks of the New York Police Department to become Inspector and Commander of Operations. After 25 years, he retired from the NYPD. In 1968, he became police commissioner in Detroit. Later, he was elected sheriff of Oakland County, and for 12 years, he was the only Democrat at the county level.

As police reporter for the *Times Herald*, I met the "Top Cop" when I was on a police-scooter assignment story back in the 1970s. You see, it was Johannes who started scooter patrols in New York City and Detroit. He also assisted Washington, D.C., police with their scooter program.

I covered several stories with him when he was sheriff, too. Our admiration and respect for each other were real. He was a class act then and he still is.

The book Johannes sent me, *American Police Dilemma—Protectors or Enforcers?* is a series of letter chapters dedicated to his daughter, Elizabeth Diane "Betty" Spreen, his late wife,

Elinor, his wife, Sallie Ann Spreen, and their grandchildren. It could be a bible, a working tool of information today, for every police officer throughout the country. The book describes how policing has gradually emphasized law enforcement over the protection of people.

Johannes pulls no punches when he looks at politics, crime control, leadership, mental and physical conditioning, morals and rivalries that reduce the effectiveness of the police officer on the street. He definitely presents a convincing case for community-oriented policing.

Who said Johannes is retired? Why, even in retirement the Big Fellow has always been the tip of the spear in every challenge that has come his way.

Laura L. Newsome, executive director of the St. Clair County Council on Aging, Inc., said Johannes is a model for growing older and a teacher in "How to Age Positively."

He was named St. Clair County's Outstanding Senior Citizen in 1999. At 83, he still teaches body recall, memory improvement and conversational German. He is also a substitute teacher at Algonac High School.

By the way, he gave me one of those life lessons of his in that race-walking competition I mentioned earlier. Johannes took the gold. I came in a bruised second. But like he said, it was nip and tuck all the way, a great race.

Maybe it's time to see if a rematch is in order for the Senior Citizen Olympics next year. Surely at 84, he can't keep up the pace that he's set for himself. Top Cop, Tip of the Spear—ahhh, who am I kidding? Johannes was born to lead. And he does.

In 2006, Spreen spoke to some local law enforcement chiefs in the West Valley area of Phoenix. One of them wrote the following story in *Arizona Republic*, the Phoenix area newspaper. Buckeye Police Chief Dan Saban wrote "My Turn: Community Policing Seeks to Bring People Together." Dan has become a good friend and in November 2008, he ran against the ever-popular Sheriff Joe Arpaio.

Community policing has evolved since the late 1970s

when I was a patrol officer in Mesa. Then, we started a program called Beat Profiling, which had as a goal connecting officers with residents.

It failed.

The program asked officers to reach out to citizens within our neighborhood beats. We would get out of our cars, talk with at least five residents a week, and hand out brochures about social services and crime-prevention programs.

Fortunately, today's community-policing concepts are nothing like they were 30 years ago. Chiefs of police recognize the importance of building relationships with the communities they serve. This is because community policing has been proven to reduce the crime rate. We also know that the bonds made between citizens and their officers develop feelings of trust and security.

Chiefs need to be innovative in creating their programs. Not everyone will be willing to support these efforts with time or money. What's partially to blame for this is that for many years police business became too inward-looking instead of forward-looking.

Another factor has been that team-policing concepts are often discussed but not always practiced. This must change if we are to build sustainable communities that are safe.

I'm inspired by legendary police commissioner and former sheriff Johannes Spreen, who, while working in Detroit during the tense racial times of the late 1960s, stated, "It takes a team, you and your police." His community-partnership approach encouraged people to work together, and it was successful.

Johannes Spreen weighed in on the Presidential campaign of 2008. Here are some of his reflections as the campaign progressed.

Yes, indeed, one must beware the "ides" of any month, particularly the October before the election. We now have the Presidential rollout of candidates for 2008. It is only the spring of 2007. The American citizen will have to bear up or brace up for many more months until November 2008. And two candidates may have already bitten the political dust. Senator John Kerry already has, with his ill-worded statement: "You know education, if you make the most of it, you study hard, you do your homework, and you make an effort to be smart, you can do well. If you don't, you get stuck in Iraq."

In February, the *New York Times* had a page one headline "Biden Unwraps His Bid of '08 with an Oops!" His spoken words may indeed have derailed his "presidential train" at the very start, before the wheels have even started to roll. These were his words at the kickoff as a candidate for the presidency, describing Senator Barack Obama, the Illinois Democrat running for president, as "the first mainstream African-American who is articulate and bright and clean and a good-looking guy."

Immediately Jesse Jackson and Al Sharpton, both African-Americans who have run for president, took issue with Mr. Biden's remarks, particularly over the words "clean" and "articulate" and "first."

Yes, as Rudyard Kipling wrote, "Words are, of course, the most powerful drug used by mankind." And like a bad drug, words can end one's political life. John Kerry knows that! Now Senator Joe Biden knows! And remember Howard Dean who let his emotions get the best of him when speaking in public?

And we all remember former President Bill Clinton's impeachment trial with his statement about the definition of "is." What is "is"??? His political career barely survived.

When the election results were announced, Spreen said, "I'm glad I'm alive for this historic event of Obama's election."

Culminating his lifetime as a lawman, he recently summer up his views about policing.

Today our police are mostly enforcers, responding to calls for service, which include many calls about troublemakers and those in their clutches. Sure, that's necessary but it's mostly after-the-fact crime.

That is my considered opinion, after many years, in the study and practice of policing. I used the term policing rather than law enforcement because police must be more than just enforcers of the laws. They must equally be preventers of crime and preservers of the peace and order of a community.

In addition to these 44 years of actual practice in police work, I have since 1985 devoted myself to thinking about police, reading about police and writing about police. This is what I sincerely believe:

We must allow our police to be much more than enforcers who get begrudging respect. We must allow our police to be seen by the citizens they serve as their protectors who deserve respect.

Why do American police get little or no respect? It's in the nature of the constraints imposed on them. Police are straitjacketed in an imposing vehicle of glass and steel. This makes them impersonal to good citizens, hardly known as humane beings.

In my first book, *American Police Dilemma,* near the conclusion, I bring out the concept of Protectors versus Enforcers. On the cover of the book are the scales of justice, tilted heavily in favor of enforcers. We must right the balance.

I now suggest we change police work. We need a different approach. We must include another type of policing, a preventive and protective role. We need policing effort *before* the fact as well as *after* the fact. I suggest that all over America, police administrators adopt "Dual Purpose Policing." That word is "dual," not "duel." There should be no struggle between contending parties.

In the past, some police departments have experimented with what was termed "Split Force Policing," realizing the distinction between response policing and preventive policing. However, the term "split" implies a separation into parts, to divide into groups or factions, to divide, to break apart. This is not good and can cause enmity and dissension.

Dual Purpose Policing could be compared to the word "dual," "duality," or "dualism." The principles of enforcement and protection can be embraced in dualism, and Dual Purpose Police Departments. Duality means Dual Controls, two-fold or double character in policing. In philosophy, "dualism" connotes the two parts of a person into mind and body. In police work, we might consider the mind as the thinking about response *before the fact* (prevention.) The body could be considered the response *after the fact* (enforcement.) Both need to be put together to work smoothly, to work in cooperation, each respecting the other, and contributing to a smooth police department process. I hope that there will be a renewed role of the citizen and taxpayer in the fight against crime. Law enforcement executives like sheriffs and police chiefs need the cooperation of the public.

Crime, disorder and vandalism are threats to our American society. Law enforcement is on the wrong path. We must use the concept and value of the old foot patrol officers in a different way. This would reduce costs and allow more visibility and opportunities to make him or her more available to the community—to really "serve and protect."

September 11, 2001, brought home a shocking fact. Three thousand killed, yes, but the real shock was that war came to America's shores. Then soon after, the snipers and hysteria on the Eastern seaboard showed that in all instances, local police and county sheriffs as well as the fire service are the first responders to all kinds of emergencies. Therefore, we must understand what is wrong with those systems of law enforcement and why we have so much trouble responding effectively. If we do respond effectively, we will earn the respect of the public. If we don't, we don't deserve respect.

We lose respect for our physicians when they don't want to talk with us about our problems but simply write prescriptions and order things that affect our very lives.

Spreen was in the forefront of movements to put police officers closer to people by using vehicles other than police cars. He introduced scooters and then recommended a return to bicycles or to the new invention—Segways.

Much to his credit and foresight, the nearest police department to Spreen's Arizona home, Surprise Police Department, adopted the Segway in 2006. They had planned to use it for crowd control at special events. However, with gas prices going sky high the need for increased summer enforcement expanded the economical vehicle's use. In June 2008, Surprise officers hit the streets on foot, on bicycles, in patrol cars and on the Segway.

The Police Department spokesperson, Sgt. Mark Ortega, said it allowed an officer easy access to greenbelt areas in communities, something a patrol car would be unable to do. That means more of the community is covered in less time. Officers have found that residents gravitate toward it due to curiosity. "We're actively making a presence in the community," said Officer Adam Muntian. Muntian was preparing to head to a major shopping area to investigate reports of juveniles harassing passers-by and causing property damage. It was ideal to dispatch the Segway since it is quiet.

The origins and success of the motor scooters as Spreen developed them in New York City was astounding, even after much derision. "Macho" cops looked with disdain at this small two-wheeled vehicle in the beginning. They preferred motorcycles. They did not understand that the motorcycle, which is good for escorts and chasing speeders, is a two-wheeled "pursuit and punitive" machine. The motor scooter is a "protective patrol vehicle." The physical difference is that a rider straddles a motorcycle like a cowboy on a horse, but a rider sits in a motor scooter and puts his legs in front of his seat as he wheels about the city.

The history and results of scooters in the City of New York, first for parks and then for city street patrols, was covered in a 1966 article Spreen wrote for the *Journal of Criminal Law, Criminology and Police Science* published by the Northwestern University School of Law. The article was entitled "The Motor Scooter—An Answer to a Police Problem".

It has been a fascinating time for Spreen to enjoy the fact that something he introduced so long ago has received praise as a better practice for current problems.

Praise for Spreen

"I'm inspired by legendary police commissioner and former sheriff Johannes Spreen, who, while working in Detroit during the tense racial times of the late 1960s stated, 'It takes a team, you and your police.' His community-partnership approach encouraged people to work together, and it was successful." Buckeye Police Chief Dan Saban

"I was accorded the priceless gift of serving with Commissioner Spreen as a New York City Police Department officer, sergeant, lieutenant, and captain. As we studied together for higher rank, I was most impressed with his ability to speak and write in a manner that produced understanding and other beneficial results. These attributes are certain to bring forth a book which, in the light of Commissioner Spreen's broad experiences, will enrich the lives of readers who are part of, or in support of, the field of criminal justice." William J. McCullough, Colonel, U.S. Army; President, Loose-leaf Law Publications; and author of *Minuteman/Activist* and *Hold Your Audience.*

"Johannes Spreen was a police officer extraordinary; a man who helped restructure and develop New York City Police Academy training leading to a college program, a 'West Point' for police officers—now John Jay College for Criminal Justice. Johannes Spreen is a man of enthusiasm, indeed a prophet; always ahead of his time and a friend for over 60 years." Rudolph P. Blaum, Retired Captain, New York City Police Department, served in the operation and development of the New York Police Service College Program, now John Jay College. He is Former President of the American Education Association in Center Moriches, New York.

"Johannes Spreen has extraordinary credentials and a range of knowledge that will achieve great results." Dr. Isaiah "Ike" McKinnon, Former Detroit Chief of Police, and Professor, University of Detroit, Mercy.

"Thanks for your dedicated service. Very nice indeed." Sheriff Joe Arpaio, Maricopa County, Arizona. *"To somebody who knows more than what's written here and who's lived through it all."* Professor Len Sherman, co-author of Sheriff Arpaio's book, *America's Toughest Sheriff.*

*"I want to take this opportunity to thank you very sincerely for the help you have given me and our own Police Chief while you were in office in Detroit. The scooter patrol innovation that you instituted in the 12*th *pre-*

cinct worked effectively for you, and based upon your recommendations, we here in Flint utilized it to a great advantage." Mayor Donald R. Cronin of Flint, Michigan

"It's almost incredible the task you faced coming to Detroit as Police Commissioner exactly one year after the disaster which this little book describes. The fact that a year later you had achieved such major break-throughs in building a bridge between the police and Detroit citizens, and healing many of the wounds within the Department, makes your tenure as Detroit's Police Commissioner one of the most significant in the city's history. We remember you with gratitude." Rev. Dr. Hubert Locke, author of *The Detroit Riot of 1967.*

"We have always felt here at the Greater Detroit Chamber of Commerce that you were the man to guide us out of the wilderness of law and order problems. Our committees and the members of the staff have enjoyed greatly their association with you. We have admired your work and hope the new innovations you introduced and ideas you developed will continue to contribute effectively to the situation here in Detroit." Dwight Havens, President of the Greater Detroit Chamber of Commerce

"I felt an obligation to tell you that I think you performed an outstanding service for the community of Detroit. So many times people in public service seem to get nothing but abuse. To me you gave every indication of dedication to your profession.

The causes of crime are pride, greed, envy, and lust. To eradicate these is more in line with my work than yours and if there is greater love of God among our people then crime will lessen. Once a man looks upon his fellow man as a person created by God and knows he must live that way then he will treat his neighbor as one of noble birth regardless of the color of his skin or the size of his bankroll. Poverty of this world's goods may be one thing which helps a person to find riches in crime but I do know for certain that poverty of the love of God causes crime." Father William Breandan of St. Dominic's Church, Detroit.

"Detroit has lost a police administrator of uncommon vision and ability." Lawrence Carino, General Manager of the WJBR-TV2 station, delivering an editorial on his station after Spreen resigned as Detroit Police Commissioner.

Appendix I

The New Yorker article, Feb. 5, 1966

"Tactical Scooter Units—TSU"

"The radio-equipped motor scooter is a comparatively slow-moving protective device that fills the gap between the foot patrolman, who covers a neighborhood in depth but cannot always get to the scene of a crime fast enough, and the patrol car, which moves rapidly but has a limited field of observation. Scooters provide mobility and flexibility. They reduce the opportunity for crime, because they can reach any part of a precinct in a matter of minutes." This pithy pronouncement was made to us by Inspector Johannes Spreen, the man in charge of the experimental motor-scooter program launched last summer by the Police Department.

The scooters have proved so effective in dealing with parking violations and with crime on the streets that the Department has decided to expand the program, and the 1966 budget has asked for funds with which to acquire a total of 685 scooters, the present total being 59. The expansion has included a nod in the direction of Johannes Spreen, a huge, rather rumpled-looking man who, as a captain and later as a deputy inspector, fought for the scooter program over a period of five years; as a sign of his and its success, he was promoted to full inspector late in November.

"Scooters have been used in Central Park and Prospect Park for the past two years," Inspector Spreen told us. "At the moment, we have nine scooters patrolling the parks, 30 on traffic duty in midtown Manhattan, and 20 assigned to what we call our Tactical Scooter Units, for experimental work. Each T.S.U. consists of seven men and six Vespas—the spare man fills in when a regular rider is off duty, sick, or in court. The men wear the usual police uniform, plus a light-blue Fiberglass helmet, and they have a two-way Motorola radio slung over the shoulder, and carry a nightstick, either in the hand or fitted into a rack on the Vespa.

"The scooter man is basically a more mobile foot patrolman. He takes his orders direct from the precinct house, unlike the radio prowl car, which is controlled by a borough-wide communications unit. The scooter itself is very nimble. It can weave through stalled traffic, jump the curb and travel along the sidewalk, cut through a narrow alley, and patrol a park that is chockablock with benches and playground equipment. Moreover, it is relatively cheap. I estimate that a man on a scooter, which costs us $300, and equipped with a two-way radio, which costs us $700, can patrol from 10 to 15 foot posts in a quarter of an hour. We may never be able to afford sufficient manpower to put a policeman on every corner, but, with scooters, we can have a policeman coming around every corner. This could cut our crime rate by as much as 30%."

Inspector Spreen suggested that we watch an experimental T.S.U. in action, and soon we found ourself in the back of an unmarked patrol car with Sgt. James P. Marron, of the Central Park scooter squad, who had been assigned to evaluate the unit. The unit was operating, for the first time, in the Seventh Precinct, on the lower East Side; on this occasion, only four of the scooter men happened to be on hand, the others being off duty (the unit operates from 10 a.m. to 6 p.m. seven days a weeks) or in court to testify on arrests made earlier in the week.

Sgt. Marron said the four men, working in pairs, would have to patrol the entire precinct, an area of about 20 blocks. "At first, they'll be working out sweep patterns," he said. "This helps them to learn the neighborhood and also to test the reception on their radios—sometimes we run into dead spots. In any event, we like to keep them moving around as much as possible; we think they reduce crime simply by being so visible."

Sgt. Marron's car was equipped to pick up scooter calls, and the first call we heard was for Scooter 20 to check on a noisy motor reported to be outside 54 Ludlow Street. By the time our car reached that address, Scooters 20 and 59 were parked at the curb, and the men had dismounted and were rapping on the windows of an enormous refrigerator truck, who motor was indeed making a fearful racket. The scootermen roused the driver, who was taking a snooze, and advised him to move his truck along to a non-residential area.

As they remounted, another radio call ordered them to the site of a sidewalk injury, at 94 Orchard Street. Our car followed the scooters as far as the corner of Canal and Orchard Streets, where a trailer truck that had failed to round a sharp turn was blocking the intersection. The scooters nipped up onto the sidewalk and disappeared down the street. The trailer truck eventually unscissored itself and freed the intersection; by then the scootermen had long since reached 94 Orchard Street, and we found them giving first aid to a young truck driver who had injured himself in an unloading accident.

In the course of the next couple of hours, the scootermen flagged down a woman who had driven through a red light, and handed her a summons; broke up a disorderly group of wine-bibbers at the corner of Suffolk and Broome Streets; checked a complaint by a woman that her black raincoat had been spattered with paint from a painter's bucket standing on a windswept scaffold; and completed a special sweep of the warehouse district down by the river—a favorite dumping ground for stolen automobiles.

We were just about to call it a day when Sgt. Marron's radio crackled into life and we heard one of the scootermen asking precinct headquarters for a license-plate check of two automobiles parked on Monroe Street. A few minutes later, the precinct dispatcher reported that one of the plates belonged to a stolen car. "Mobility and good communications," Sgt. Marron said. "That's what it takes, and that's what the scooters give us."

References

Adler, Freda et al. *Criminology,* 2nd Ed. McGraw-Hill, Inc.: New York, 1995.

Alderson, John. *Law and Disorder*. Hamish Hamilton: London, 1984.

Alderson, John. (with Philip John Stead, Ed.) *The Police We Deserve*, Wolfe Publishing: London, 1973.

Alderson, John. *Policing Freedom*, Macdonald and Evans: London, 1979.

Bayley, David H. *Police for the Future*. Oxford University Press: New York, 1994.

Devlin, Patrick. *The Enforcement of Morals*. Oxford University Press: London, 1965.

McIntyre, Tommy. *Wolf in Sheep's Clothing: The Search for a Child Killer*. Wayne State University Press, 1988.

Spreen, Johannes with Holloway, Diane. *American Police Dilemma: Enforcers or Protectors?* New York: iUniverse, Inc., 2003.

Spreen, Johannes with Holloway, Diane. *American Law Enforcement Does Not Serve or Protect*. New York: iUniverse, Inc., 2004.

Spreen, Johannes and Holloway, Diane. *Who Killed Detroit: Other Cities Beware!* New York: iUniverse, Inc., 2005.

Spreen, Johannes and Lee, Cherie. *The Saga of Thundercloud and Dancing Star*. New York: iUniverse, Inc., 2006.

About the Author

Diane Holloway, Ph.D. was a Dallas psychologist, and was appointed the first Drug "Czar" of Dallas by the Mayor. She also helped the Dallas Police Department develop their first police assessment center for upper ranks in 1987-1988. She was an associate member of the International Association of Chiefs of Police, a member of the American Psychological Association, and served as a consultant to fire, police and city governments across the country. Earlier she was a management consultant and trainer on personnel selection with some of America's largest corporations.

She wrote, co-authored, and edited books with Johannes Spreen, Ken Jacuzzi, James MacLeod, Judge Joe B. Brown, Dr. Don Farrior, Fred Brown III, Lois Gentry, Nancy Bishop, Bob Cheney, William Dullas, Jerry Moriarity, Edna M. Collins, and many others.

She wrote *Before You Say 'I Quit'*; *The Mind of Oswald; American History in Song; Dallas and the Jack Ruby Trial; Analyzing Leaders, Presidents and Terrorists, Who Killed New Orleans*, and edited *Autobiography of Lee Harvey Oswald*.

She and co-authors, Johannes Spreen and Bob Cheney, won first place for non-fiction in the Arizona Authors Association Annual Contest for *Who Killed New Orleans? Mother Nature vs. Human* Nature published in 2005.

www.ingramcontent.com/pod-product-compliance
Lightning Source LLC
Chambersburg PA
CBHW061348280526
45784CB00001B/185